Anxiety & Pregnancy:
31 Useful Tips To Manage Anxiety During & After Pregnancy

By Sophie Acker

Contents

Introduction

For the most part, pregnancy talk is focused around the growing fetus. The proper amount of nutrients it needs, the necessary vitamins and the best way to ensure a healthy, strong birth. However, while all of these aspects are central to a successful pregnancy, the mother's mental health is also a very important aspect to this process. When you are pregnant, your levels of distress can have negative effects on your baby. In order to teach how to combat these effects, this guide will outline different ways to cope with distress as it occurs during pregnancy, and this introduction will explain why controlling that distress is so important.

Distress during pregnancy comes in a variety of forms, which can include anxiety, stress and depression. Remember, a pregnant mother is always connected to her baby. The mother constantly fuels the growing fetus, supplying it with the different nutrients and vitamins it needs to survive. In the same way, if the mother is under stress or suffering from depression, the fetus may also be affected. This could cause complications with the baby once it is born, and even create longer lasting effects throughout the child's life. However, by knowing and understanding the ways to handle different types of distress, those complications can be mitigated, or even avoided altogether.

One of the foremost factors that can lead to a complicated pregnancy is anxiety. As a pregnant woman, it is natural to feel anxiety, stress or even fear. These are understandable reactions to a very new, and somewhat overwhelming situation. Even so, anxiety, which will be discussed in further detail later, can be very harmful to a birth. Small levels of anxiety are quite normal, but if that anxiety reaches it can become quite harmful. High levels of anxiety in pregnant woman can negatively influence the development of a fetus, and can even cause things such as low birth weight or prematurity.

Besides the level or severity of distress, the stage at which said distress occurs is also important in understanding the way a baby can be affected. For instance, controlling distress, while always important, is particularly key during the early stages of pregnancy. Any form of distress, which can include things such as depression, anxiety or stress, can have lasting, long-term effects on a baby's growth both in the womb and after. This is due to the fact that, if a mother experiences high levels of this distress while in the first trimester, it can stunt neurological and behavioral development during the early stages of that child's life.

By averting distress, these complications can be avoided, which in turn can lead to a healthier child and more successful birth. It is always important to be aware of your stress levels during pregnancy, and do what you can to keep them under control. These after-birth complications are one of the primary reasons that preventing distress is so important, but they are not the only reason. Just how distress in the early stages can affect a child after their birth, anxiety and stress seen in the later stages of pregnancy can also cause problems for the mother as well.

In late pregnancy, high levels of distress can be damaging to mothers, as it can make them much more susceptible to postpartum depression. This depression can be a very serious issue, and cause problems to the relationship between the mother and child. As such, it is something that birthing mothers should do their best to prevent. Having high distress levels during late stages does not necessarily mean a mother will develop postpartum depression, but it does make them at a much higher risk. However, this is also a prime example of why controlling distress during pregnancy is so important for the sake of both the mother and child. Don't forget, pregnancy is a two-way street, a relationship that exists between the mother and her unborn infant. Things that harm one part of that relationship, be they physical or mental, commonly harm the other.

In addition to creating problems both during and after birth, anxiety can also cause complications in the relationship between the mother and a newborn infant. Just as when in the womb, an infant's relationship with their mother is very important to stimulating proper growth. If this relationship is damaged or harmed in any way, it could cause problems in a child's early development, and may even have lasting effects throughout their life. This shows why distress is so important to control, as it can negatively affect birth, pregnancy, the mother, the child and even the relationship the two have after birth.

All of these problems and possible complications may seem daunting at first glance, but they are merely discussed in this introduction to show the importance of the practices and tips that will be outlined in the following pages. Each section of this guide will cover different methods to properly deal with and prepare for the distress that can occur during pregnancy. Remember, there are many methods in these pages. So, if you find that one way does not work for you, know that there are plenty of other options available, and try one of those.

Pregnancy is by no means an easy process, but it can be very manageable with the proper knowledge and preparation. This guide will not only ensure you have a successful pregnancy, but it will also show you how to ensure you have a healthy baby as well. As a mother, you want the best for your baby, and you also want to make sure it has the best chance at life. That is a battle that begins long before birth, and it starts with knowing how to properly control the stress, anxiety and depression that can happen during the different stages throughout your pregnancy.

1. The CALM Pregnancy Program

The very first method that we will cover in this guide is one of the many ways to handle the natural anxiety that can come from pregnancy. Anxiety is one of the most common types of distress that can occur during this time, and using this method is a great way to reduce it. This method of handling anxiety is called Coping with Anxiety through Living Mindfully, or CALM.

CALM is an adaptation of mindfulness based cognitive therapy (commonly referred to as MBCT) that was designed with the sole purpose of lessening anxiety during the pregnancy process. There are several parts of the CALM method, and each one is central to making the process work. Each of these practices will be laid out below, as will their importance to the entire method as a whole. Each of these practices all fall under different, broader categories, and they will all be explained as well.

The first thing you must understand when practicing the CALM method, is that there are five different categories of help. Each of these is a personal practice you yourself must do in order to receive the full benefits of the method. The categories in question are psychoeducation, mindfulness practices, cognitive exercises, home practice and reading material. If you manage to do all of the activities related to these, you will have a great chance of cutting back on your anxiety and stopping the negative effects that stem from distress.

Psychoeducation is the first, and one of the most important, methods of CALM that you should use. Psychoeducation is a term that refers to having knowledge about the different methods you are performing. That is to say, what mindfulness is, why it is so import, and the different ways it can help you. Practicing mindfulness also falls under this category, as does understanding stress physiology, anxiety and depression. Your mind a powerful tool when it comes to staying healthy, and you cannot properly fight these ailments without first understanding how they work.

Mindfulness is a way to respond to anxiety that differs from more traditional models, and is a method that is central to the entire CALM practice. In conventional pregnancy practices, anxiety is avoided at all costs. However, with mindfulness, anxiety is deliberately noticed, and even allowed. Once this happens, the anxiety is then responded to with a sense of acceptance. This may seem strange, as anything that fights conventional wisdom is, but it is through accepting the anxiety that will allow you to overcome this form of distress.

Through accepting the anxiety as it comes, you create a much higher level of behavioral flexibility, which is a central part of being able to adapt to different situations as they arise. This even helps cut back on stress. People who have practiced mindfulness have shown, through compiled data, clinically significant improvements with both worrying and depression in addition to the reduction of anxiety. This is a huge part of CALM, but it is not the only aspect of using mindfulness to cut back on overall anxiety.

As part of the psychoeducation process, you should also familiarize yourself with how mindfulness can be utilized throughout the different stages of pregnancy. Each part of CALM has a particular purpose, and mindfulness should be used in every way that it can when you are faced with a problem. From the very beginning of the pregnancy all the way to the birth, mindfulness should be practiced in labor, delivery and even parenting, in order to help you adapt to new and unfamiliar situations.

Beyond the initial phase of psychoeducation, another integral part to CALM is actually applying the different types of mindfulness to your normal life. At its core, mindfulness is accepting anxiety, and then using that acceptance to cope. However, there are also a number of different mindfulness practices that can be used as ways to further combat anxiety as it happens. While using mindfulness in everyday life has already been covered, you can also use both meditation (sitting and walking) in addition to yoga. Both of these will help you remain calm. Baby practices and body scans are also good ways to keep a sense of peace throughout your pregnancy.

The next stage of CALM, which are also good practices when dealing with anxiety, are cognitive exercises. Just as with the different mindfulness practices, these methods are things you can do on your own to improve the way you react to different situations.

The first cognitive exercise is self-observation in conjunction with self-monitoring. Both of these refer to skill development, and, similar to meditation, will help you gain peace through a better understanding of who you are. Self-compassion meditation, which is a variation on traditional compassion meditation, is one cognitive exercise that is very helpful in reaching this goal. However, instead of focusing on other people, this meditation is built around building compassion for yourself. This will help your journey through pregnancy, and can build off of the central idea in mindfulness by allowing you to get a better understanding of yourself. The other cognitive exercise you should do as a part of CALM is decentering from automatic thoughts. What this means is, you want to try and think more about your first impulses before acting on them. Learn to recognize what thoughts are harmful, why they are harmful, and how those realizations can help your overall mental health.

Another mode of CALM is home practicing. Most of the methods listed above are things you either go somewhere to do, or are things you can practice while going about your daily life. However, when at home it is natural to relax and forget about your practices. In order to avoid this, it is a good idea to try and practice mindfulness at home thirty to forty five minutes a day, six days a week. This is beneficial, as it will not only help those practices become more refined, but the repetition will also make them feel a lot more natural until they become a part of your daily routine.

Sources: *Goodman et al., Arch Womens Ment Health. 2014; 17:373*

2. Peer Support Therapy

In the next section, we will switch modes to look at data related to another form of controlling distress, therapy. It is often a good idea for pregnant woman to find a place where they can share or talk about any problems or feelings they might be having. This is a great way to offset distress, and try to keep calm during a turbulent time. Doubt, depression and stress can all be mitigated by being able to openly discuss any problems you might experience.

Both psycho and cognitive therapy are means to helping a woman through pregnancy, and each has had some very positive results. Each method is particularly effective as a way to combat both anxiety as well as prenatal depression. However, while these methods are quite effective, they can also be expensive, and are not always affordable for woman undergoing the already costly process of pregnancy. If you are one of these women, or if you just do not want to pay for therapy, fear not. Data, which will be covered below, has shown that there is a worthy alternative to therapy that is cheap, easy and is just as effective at battling stress. This alternative is engaging in peer support groups rather than seeing a professional therapist.

Peer support group sessions are exactly as they sound: therapy sessions that are run by peers rather than by trained professionals. This may sound a little off putting at first, but it has been shown to be a good way for woman who cannot afford traditional therapy to still receive the benefits. Not only that, but the data referenced below shows that this type of peer-run therapy has very similar benefits to therapy run by a therapist. It is not who you are necessarily speaking to that matters, as long as you are speaking to someone who understands and is willing to listen.

In order to properly show the benefits of peer support groups, we will outline a study that was conducted to test their effectiveness. This study compared the effect of traditional psychotherapy to peer therapy, and then examined the results each had on a group of pregnant women. In one group, pregnant woman underwent therapy with an active therapist for an hour a day over twelve weeks' time. In contrast, another group of pregnant woman took part in a meeting where the staff member was not a trained therapist. These sessions went for a total of twelve weeks as well, and these sessions were twenty minutes long, and happened just once a week. Then, the women in each group were tested on their levels of anxiety, depression and anger. The mean scores of these results were taken down and then compared to their levels at the end of the twelve weeks.

Conventional logic would tell us that, in the study, the woman who took place in the group that was run by an active therapist would have seen a greater drop in anxiety than those who went to the peer support group. Not only was this not the case, but it seems that the success of each group was very similar at the end of the trial. Each group saw a drop in both anxiety and depression, which reveals the effectiveness that a peer support group can have.

Looking at the three categories (depression, anger and anxiety) each group had their own numbers of women suffering from each. The mean score for depression (CES-D) in the first group was 20.0 and the depressed affect was 9.9. After going through psychotherapy with a trained therapist, these numbers dropped to 17.5 and 6.4 respectively. When it came to anxiety, the starting mean was 41.3, which fell to 38.7. However, anger started out at 17.3 and then had a slight increase to 17.6. Despite the increase in anger, this does show the effectiveness of therapy for pregnant woman, and how going to such a group can be beneficial for your mental health.

When comparing the results of the study, depression for women in the peer support group started at 26.8 and fell to 21.0, and the depressed affect started at 10.1 and went to 6.7. The anxiety went from 48.5 to 43.2 and, unlike the psychotherapy group led by an active therapist, the mean for anger in this group actually dropped, from 19.2 to 18.1. This shows the peer support group was just as, if not more, effective than the psychotherapy group. Yes, this is simply data from one study, but it also shows the progress that going to a group can have.

The above data shows that peer support group sessions may be as effective as interpersonal psychotherapy. These groups can be a good way to reduce both anxiety and depression seen in pregnant women, and can also help you mitigate distress during the entire process. If you ever find yourself isolated or feeling alone, try and find a group that works for you.

This study is brought up, not to prove that one style of therapy session is any better than the other, but rather to show how the peer support group is an effective alternative method. The most important factor to take away, beyond that you should always find some form of support to talk to during pregnancy, is there are many options available to you. Pregnancy, in addition to being a stressful or daunting process, can also be expensive. However, this should not worry you, as there are affordable ways to relieve your distress without having to pay too much. Peer support groups are one of these great alternatives.

Sources: *Field et al., Early Human Development. 2013; 89:621*

3. Singing During Pregnancy

While there are many more traditional treatments that will be covered throughout this guide, one of the more unconventional methods that can be an effective way to combat distress is through singing. Singing, more accurately singing lullabies, has been proven to have positive effects for both the mother as well as the growing baby.

The first reason singing during pregnancy is so important, is that it can be a great way to reduce distress. This stems from its ability to create many benefits for a pregnant mother. Having less problems, or are simply suffering less than normal, can make living while pregnant much easier. At its base, singing is something anyone can do, and it serves as a great way to connect with your unborn baby.

Singing is a very powerful method when trying to control both anxiety and stress. However, what makes it a good suggestion for any new mother, is the ease with which it can be done. Singing is very easy to implement, and something you can quickly build into your daily routine alongside your other daily practices. While there are many different types of singing, as mentioned you should try to sing lullabies. Lullabies are the best type of singing, as their calm tone can help soothe you. Not only that, but they also build a deeper connection between you and your baby. Lullabies have even been shown to greatly reduce maternal stress, which can be very common throughout pregnancy, in addition to encouraging infant attachment.

Lullabies are also important in that they can aid the proper development of a growing fetus, which aids in helping attachment after birth. When the baby grows in the womb, they do not start to develop hearing until 25 or 26 weeks into gestation. At this point, their ear drums begin to form. At this point, even while they are still inside their mother, an infant has the ability to hear. It is here where a mother's voice can be both heard and recognized by the baby. It is at this stage where you should begin to start singing lullabies.

Babies, even in the womb, have the ability to recognize their mother's voice. The prenatal exposure that is caused through singing is a great way to develop a bond with your baby during the months that they are first being developed. As such, re-exposure to their mother's voice after the birthing process actually furthers attachment. This happens more quickly to singers, as their children already recognize the voice. Earlier in this guide we covered how stress can lead to a dissociation between a mother and child, but these lullabies are one of the best ways to prevent that dissociation from ever occurring.

Another strong benefit of singing to your baby while they are still in the womb, is it can contribute to positive maternal infant interaction. Maternal infant interaction is another element of creating a successful bond between mother and child. If you are anxious or nervous about having the proper attachment, lullabies are a great way to ease that stress. Many woman have used singing as way to calm their own anxiety about connecting with their baby. These practices are a great way to reduce maternal stress, which in turn leads to a better, easier pregnancy.

Lullaby singing has shown many benefits throughout its use. Of these benefits is connecting with your husband, connecting with your infant and helping you feel closer to your baby. This practice also helps pregnant mother's find their own voice, and gives them confidence. It also can be very relaxing. Just as the baby may become more connected to the mother, this process has also shown to make mothers feel much more connected to their baby as well. If you are feeling detachment, or are nervous about how to properly talk or interact with your baby, this type of lullaby singing is a very good route to take while pregnant.

Sources: *Carolan et al., Midwifery. 2012; 28:173*

4. Yoga

This section will cover something we previously touched upon in the guide about wellness practices. This is the implementation of yoga during pregnancy. Outside of the pregnancy sphere, yoga is a very popular exercise. It is a very good practice that is very calming, soothing, and has been even shown to relieve stress. These benefits come from many different elements, such as giving users a break from their normal life. That is an important element to relaxation, and yoga has the added benefit of helping to strengthen your body as well. In addition, Tai Chi, another practice that will be covered in this section, is a very good way to keep your body healthy as you progress through different trimesters. Similar to yoga, Tai Chi is built on many practices that are very good for woman trying to stay healthy during their pregnancy. Here, we will take a look at how the linking of body and mind that occurs during both Tai Chi and yoga can be very important to a successful pregnancy period.

Both of the methods are very helpful to pregnancy, because they both teach balance, poise and can provide you with a peaceful, relaxing space. While this section will individually look at the benefits of each practice, you should remember that it is always good to combine them into a schedule that works for you. Just as with the aforementioned methods, a combination of yoga and Tai Chi have been shown to garner numerous benefits for pregnant woman. These include a decrease in both anxiety and depression as well as a drop in sleep disturbances. However, rather than waiting for any of these ailments, it is better to work yoga and Tai Chi into your normal routine as a way to make sure they never happen. A study (*Field et al., Complementary Therapies in Clinical Practice. 2013; 19:6*) conducted with 92 pregnant women, showed that yoga and Tai Chi, while strong on their own, have a plethora of benefits when practiced together. Just as with singing, Tai Chi may not be the first thing that comes to your mind when you think of good pregnancy practices. However, the values that it teaches can be very beneficial to pregnant women. One of the most important of these values is balance. As your pregnancy progresses, your body will begin to change. This can affect balance, and make it more difficult to move in the way that you are used to. Not only that, but this change could also make you more prone to falling or stumbling when moving around. Falling can be detrimental to pregnancy, and should be avoided at all costs. An increase in balance can help you avoid falling by allowing you to better live and move with your new form. Balance is a large part of Tai Chi, and that balance will make you much more aware of your own space. This is one of the most effective ways to lower your risk of falling.

Yoga works very well as a calming practice for any mother, but it is especially relevant during the early stages of your pregnancy. This is a time where you are much slimmer and more limber, which allows you to gain the full benefits of the process. Now, that is not to say yoga is ineffective during the later stages, where it can still be used to relaxation, but it just isn't as easy to do. Yoga is an exercise that helps with many different ailments you can experience by connecting your body and mind. However, it also requires a lot of different stretching and poses. If you find that you cannot perform these poses due to your progressing pregnancy, then it could be a good idea to focus more of your attention towards Tai Chi.

Tai Chi is very beneficial during the later stages of pregnancy for two primary reasons. One, balance tends to become more and more important the later into pregnancy you are. As your baby grows and you become larger, it gets harder to walk and something as simple as moving can seem almost unfamiliar. Using Tai Chi can greatly improve this process by enabling you to keep upright and move around. The second reason Tai Chi can be so beneficial during the later stages of pregnancy is because yoga requires you to be limber, as stated earlier. Naturally, doing poses and balancing effectively becomes much more difficult as your baby continues to grow inside of you. As such, during your later trimesters, yoga may be too much of a risk to attempt.

When starting pregnancy, you should try to use elements of both yoga and tai chi to strengthen your body. However, yoga is primarily focused on early use. If you find it working for you, either as a space of rest or as a form of exercise, you may want to switch to Tai Chi. This allows you to continue those practices, while being able to much more easily get the help that you need without putting your body at risk.

Sources: *Field et al., Complementary Therapies in Clinical Practice. 2013; 19:6. Campbell et al., New Digest. 2010; 51:23*

5. Relationship Between Coping Strategies and Anxiety

In understanding the values and practices laid out in these pages, one of the biggest questions we need to answer is: why use coping strategies? That is a fair question to ask, and one that deserves a proper answer. Distress is not seen by every woman when she undergoes pregnancy, but it is very common. All forms of distress can range in both severity and amount. Still, even if you are only experiencing anxiety or depression in small scales, you should still do your best to fight them. Here, we will once again be taking a look at some clinical data to further understand why coping is so important to a successful pregnancy.

The study in question was a French study (*George et al., BMC Pregnancy and Childbirth. 2013; 13:23*) that was performed to analyze if coping strategies could indeed help women during the pregnancy process. We have already covered the benefits that lowering distress during pregnancy can have on a growing fetus, but what of the mother's overall mental health? As a pregnant woman, your own personal feelings are very important, and the following information should help you understand the best way to maintain a good state of mind.

In the study, researchers looked at 400 pregnant women. Throughout the study, the women were followed from the 26th-35th week of gestation, up until 6-8 weeks after childbirth. Researchers recorded the information based off of those who experienced more anxiety than others, and tracked which of the subjects used coping strategies more often.

Overall, the data revealed that women who exhibited severe or extremely damaging anxiety used coping strategies much less than woman who did not suffer from such conditions. These coping strategies included things such as acceptance (as covered in the first section of this guide) positive reframing and humor. Each one of these methods is a good way to face problems and, according to the data found by the study, all add to an overall reduction of distress. While each type of coping strategy was tested, the takeaway here is that any type of coping strategy, no matter what the exact method, helps curb levels of distress.

Besides the results that showed woman using coping mechanisms were much less likely to experience stress during pregnancy, the test also revealed another negative effect of anxiety. It showed that woman who experienced high levels of anxiety, which can be reduced through these coping mechanisms, are much more prone to problematic responses to distress. Instead of rationally approaching their problems as they come, pregnant women who suffer from anxiety used negative responses such as denial or self-blame. Both of these responses can be very detrimental to any woman going through pregnancy, which outlines yet another reason healthy responses can be so important. It also accentuates the importance of improving adaptive coping, which includes both positive reframing and acceptance.

When looking at the way the two groups of women coped, women who were anxious used much less adaptive coping responses than those who were not as anxious. This reveals yet another example of how important coping can be to a successful pregnancy. Not only that, but this data also shows the importance of a good mind set, which can be built through the right practices. This study is a good starting point, as here you can understand why the coping and adaptive methods that will follow through this guide are so important helping you along your journey. Pregnancy, as seen in the introduction, is not an easy process, but it can be made easier. The number one rule, that will permeate throughout the following sections, is you will always be better off if both your mind and body are at peace. Coping mechanisms are just one of the many ways to achieve this.

Sources: *George et al., BMC Pregnancy and Childbirth. 2013; 13:233*

6. Psychosocial Resources

For the next part of this guide, we will be looking at the way your own mental thinking can directly effect the success, or failure, of having an easy pregnancy. Both physical form and a healthy body are very important when trying to create a child, but a strong brain can be just as is important. In this way, a good, sound mind can lead to a much healthier lifestyle, which can lead to a much healthier baby. Psychosocial resources, the topic of this section, can help you by leading to many great stress-buffering effects. These effects, which will be outlined below, are great ways to cut down your overall distress.

Time and time again, self-efficacy has been associated with people's health, and this is no different in pregnant women. Self-efficacy, which is a big part of the psychosocial process, has been defined as "people's beliefs about their capabilities to produce effects". What that means is, if you believe something, it is more likely to come true. This applies to both positive and negative effects. Believe you are capable, and you are more likely to achieve your goal. In the same vein, believe you are inadequate, and you are just as likely to fail; very similar to the idea of a self-fulfilling prophecy. These thoughts can become amplified under stressful conditions, and should be carefully monitored when undergoing pregnancy. Health is directly linked to your mind, and these thoughts can have adverse effects as you move towards birth.

While there are many negative effects associated with negative thinking, the good news is, it is very easy to achieve self-efficacy. All it takes is changing your mindset. One theme that will constantly be brought up in this guide, is self-awareness. Just as in both CALM and wellness practices, you want to be cognizant of any distress you might be under. What caused it? Why are you feeling this way? This type of thinking will help you during this section, as it will allow you to better understand exactly what is going on in your mind to cause distress. Once you are aware of this, you can then work on different ways to improve it.

The most important part of improving your mindset is through daily uplifts. Daily uplifts is a term that refers to small, almost easy, tasks that will further your overall health. These can range from an assortment of different things, from spending time with your family, to receiving a compliment, to just laughing more often. A positive mindset comes from two sources that you should always try and tap into. One, it comes from maintaining a good attitude, and two, it is also built off of positive actions. These uplifts fall into the latter category, but can make a huge difference in your everyday thinking. Pregnancy can be a hard time, but as in the case of singing lullabies, working small, positive routines into your daily life will do wonders for you, which in turn will do wonders for your baby.

Self-efficacy is a great technique for pregnant woman looking to cut back on any distress they may be feeling. To show this, we will reference the results of yet another study

(*Neirop et al., Biological Psychology. 2008; 78:261*). Here, 60 pregnant women were used as subjects in a random trail. The women in question went through their normal time in pregnancy, but did so using daily uplifts as the primary form of self-efficacy. The researchers, in order to determine just how successful the effects were, then monitored the way those acts affected both anxiety as well as perceived stress. In the end, the women unanimously showed that these psychosocial resources greatly cut back on the anxiety the woman were previously showing, and the data revealed higher self-efficacy was associated with lower stress reactivity in terms of perceived stress and anxiety. The methods also greatly reduced physiological and psychological stress responses as well. This study gives you an idea of just how important your mind can be for both you and your baby. Pregnancy is a mental battle as much as it is a physical one, and you always want to keep your mind as strong as you can. Just how Tai Chi and yoga help you balance your inner self, these psychosocial practices will help you maintain a clear mind. If you can stay positive, and thus offset anxious or negative thoughts, then you are making one of the best steps you can towards moving forward. A healthy mind leads to a healthy body. Remember, it is not an easy journey, but if you think you can do it, you most likely can.

Sources: *Neirop et al., Biological Psychology. 2008; 78:261*

7. Birth Ball Exercises

As previously covered in the section regarding Tai Chi, exercise is a very good way to stay healthy during your pregnancy period. Not only will it enable you to better your balance as well as your sense of self, but it also will make you stronger and give your baby a chance at a much better start in life. Beyond using softer methods, such as yoga and Tai Chi, there are other good exercises that will help improve your physicality as well as cut back on stress. While the methods laid below will be more geared toward your physical body, every method also helps your brain, as they all pertain to reducing the amount of distress you are under. These exercises, while important in keeping a healthy body, all do this in addition to creating a more mentally sound mind. This unison will help you better deal with the coming days.

This will not be the last time we cover different exercises that are available to pregnant women, but the following is one of the most effective at cutting back on pregnancy related anxiety. That exercise is using a birth ball, which are a form of exercise or gym ball. These are great for performing many different exercises, and they can also serve as a great way to reduce your levels of distress. Exercises with birth balls have been shown to do this through reducing stress that is commonly seen in pregnant women. In addition, they have also been shown to greatly reduce anxiety, and even mitigate labor pain.

Birth balls are very good to use all throughout the pregnancy process, but can be especially important during the later stages of pregnancy. Just as in the case of yoga, the more your baby (and subsequently you) grows, it gets harder and harder to perform different exercises as well as to perform different actions. When things like yoga become too much to handle, the birth ball will still be a good way to get the exercise you need.

So, how should you use a birth ball? While there are no general guidelines, a good rule to follow is, if you're up to 5 feet 8 inches in height, you typically want to get a ball that is 65 centimeters around. However, if you are taller (5 feet 9 inches or above) then you typically want to stay with a ball that is 75 centimeters. In terms of size, a good, high-quality birth ball should be able to support you no matter what your weight, which means you should only need one size during the whole of your pregnancy.

It should come as no surprise that being pregnant can cause a lot of stress to your body. The added weight and change of posture can have adverse effects on your body if you're not careful, and stress from those effects can add to your anxiety. However, if you manage to reduce these health problems, a reduction to anxiety and stress will surely follow. It is in this way that using a birth ball can be very important to allowing your mind to remain strong.

When first using a birth ball, it is generally a good idea to work with someone who can support your from behind. This is extremely important during the later stages, when it becomes harder and harder to maintain proper balance. Using a partner to start will give you a chance to become more acclimated with using the ball, and allow you to learn how to exercise with it in a safe, risk-free environment. Also, an important thing to remember: when using a birth ball you want to either use slip-free shoes or go barefoot. This will reduce any risk of you slipping off of the ball, which can cause injury to both you and your baby. Using a spotter while using the ball will also reduce the risk of slipping.

A birth ball is also beneficial as it is a great way to improve your posture and balance. This can greatly reduce falling, which is one of the primary things you want to avoid during pregnancy. Also, working with a birth ball is a very good way to strengthen your stomach muscles. This is good for two reasons. One, it will help your body better support the extra weight of your pregnancy, which is beneficial to helping you reduce pain to your joints. Strong stomach muscles are also very good in supporting your back, which can be hurt by the added weight of pregnancy. Each of these will also allow you to keep a good balance, which in turn can make things easier to cope with. It has also been shown that strong stomach muscles make it much easier to get back into shape after the pregnancy period comes to an end.

Discussing ways to improve your body may seem like a break from talking about how to reduce distress but, just as a mother and her child are connected, so are your mind and body. If you remain healthy, it will be much easier to keep your mind in a good place. Positive affirmation, along with the psychosocial practices outlined in these pages, will also be much easier to do if you can curb any physical pain that may come up. The further into pregnancy you go, the more important it is to stay in tune with yourself. A birth ball is a great alternative method for both pain relief and stress reduction. Using birth balls have even been shown to promote relaxation in labor wards. If you are looking for a good way to reduce labor pain, or a way to improve your core and back strength, a birth ball is one of the best ways to go.

Sources: *Leung et al., Hong Kong Med J. 2013; 19:393*

8. Aromatherapy

The next practice we will look at is aromatherapy. Aromatherapy can be very beneficial as it helps all types of distress that can happen during pregnancy. Unlike most methods laid out in this guide, which tend to focus on a specific type of distress reduction, aromatherapy covers many different bases, and has been shown to have a variety of both physical and psychological effects.

This section will list a large variety of different aromas, and then explain how each of those aromas can help you. This type of medicine, which is for people who want to try different types of medication, is referred to as Complementary and Alternative Medicine, or CAM. CAM branches out to include many different types of therapies, one of which includes aromatherapy. There are many reasons one would choose CAM, but the most prevalent is to avoid negative side effects that are commonly associated with medicine.

When using aromatherapy, you want to use essential oils. These oils are the main catalyst for the process, and will give you the positive results you seek. Each different oil will be broken down in the following paragraphs, which will help you discover which ones are best for you. It should also be noted, always be careful when dealing with essential oils during pregnancy, as some oils can cause harm rather than relief. The ones below are listed to be safe.

The first essential oil that can be used is bergamot. Bergamot is very good for curbing anxiety. This is due to its calming qualities. Bergamot can also help relieve pain as well as fight off any infections you may be suffering from. It also has the ability to improve cystitis, which refers to the swelling of the bladder through bacteria, during pregnancy.

Another great essential oil is chamomile. Just like Bergamot, chamomile has the ability to reduce infection as well as inflammation. However, it also has added calming effects and can work to soothe muscle aches as well. Chamomile is a great way to treat pain, both inflammatory and digestive, and it will also help you stay calm.

Lavender, the next oil on the list, has an array of different functions. When used, lavender, like the different oils above, has the ability to help with natural aches and common pain that can come as a result of pregnancy, but it has some added effects as well. Lavender can assist with fluid retention, and causes natural states of relaxation. It can also be particularly beneficial to women suffering from depression due to its natural anti-depressant qualities.

If depression is a problem you find yourself battling with, petitgrain is a great oil for you. Petitgrain has many natural depression-fighting qualities, and should be used as such. It can even be used when treating depression that lasts after birth. This oil is both calming and soothing, and has a number of antiseptic qualities. Sandalwood also helps with depression, and, much like bergamot, is another way to lower cystitis. It is also very calming, and can be used as an anti-inflammatory.

Tangerine is the last oil of this section. Like so many other essential oils, tangerine is naturally calming, but it also holds sedative qualities. It also has the added bonus of preventing unwanted stretch marks that occur as you grow. These oils all have their benefits, and finding the best one for you is important. If you want to undergo treatment, but are worried about medicines, aromatherapy is a great alternative route.

To understand the effects of aromatherapy beyond simple oils, we will have to analyze the results from another study (*Igarashi et al., The Journal of Alternative and Complimentary Medicine. 2013; 19:805*). Here, researchers studied a number of pregnant women to examined how aromatherapy affected their responses in the 28th week of gestation . To gain data, the woman were split into two groups, one which was given aromatherapy, and one that was not. The women who were undergoing the therapy had a choice between lavender, petitgrain and bergamot oils. Those women then chose one of the three, and used that during their entire process. After the study, data concluded that aromatherapy was indeed an effective alternative method to traditional medication. All women in the study were given inhalation aromatherapy, and then monitored based on the type of oil they chose. While this is not a breakdown of each individual case, we will go over the overall results, which proves the effectiveness of the method.

All women who took place in the study showed significant improvement after undergoing the therapy. These included an improvement to mood as well as physiological relaxing effects.

All of these recorded effects also showed a decrease in all stress levels, including anger, hostility, anxiety and stress.

There are numerous reasons why this method is so successful for women, but each oil in the study shared one common link: relaxation. Linalyl acetate and linalool, two compounds that were found in all three oils, have been shown to have calming effects on people using them. This explains why the aromatherapy resulted in such a soothing effect.

When the results were compiled and put onto both the Tension-Anxiety and Anger-Hostility score, the amount of distress unanimously dropped for all women who underwent aromatherapy. The Tension-Anxiety scale showed a score reduction from 3.7 to 1.1, while the Anger-Hostility score went from 2.7 all the way to 0. These records show that aromatherapy has some serious potential for anybody who is actively seeking a way to a more natural pregnancy. Medicine, while popular, may not be for everyone. Even if you do take some medications, if they are not giving you the desired effect, aromatherapy is a ready adjunct therapy.

However, not all essentials oils used in aromatherapy are beneficial. Some oils can be harmful to you, and should be avoided during pregnancy. These are listed below.

The oils you should avoid are as follows: Arborvitae, beth root, black cohosh, blue cohosh, cascara, chaste tree berry, chinese angelic (Dong Quai), cinchona, cotton root bark, feverfew, ginseng, golden seal, juniper, kava kava, licorice, meadow saffrom, pennyroyal, poke root, rue, sage, saint johns wort, senna, tansy, white peony, wormwood, yarrow, yellowdock. Calamus oil, mugwort oil, pennyroyal oil, sage oil, wintergreen oil, basil oil, hyssop oil, myrrh oil, marjoram oil, thyme oil, birch oil, cedar oil, cinnamon oil, clove bud oil, cypress oil (not for first two trimesters), fennel oil, jasmine oil, juniper oil, lemongrass oil, parsley oil, peppermint oil and rosemary oil.

Anything not listed here may be ok to use, but check beforehand to make sure you are as safe as possible.

Sources: *Igarashi et al., The Journal of Alternative and Complimentary Medicine. 2013; 19:805*

9. Medication and Side Effects

Though we have been looking a lot of alternative methods of pregnancy stress reduction, it would not be fair to not mention medicine. Medicine is one of the ways to fight through the distress that occurs during pregnancy. Medicine has shown to be an effective way to combat your problems, but there are also a number of risks associated with different, popular types. However, it is important to remember that stopping medication or not taking it as indicated, may cause serious relapse, and may do greater harm to you and your child. For this reason, always talk to your doctor before changing your treatment plan. For advice, you can discuss your concerns not only with your physician or OB-GYN, but finding a psychiatrist who specializes in treating pregnant women, may help you should more serious anxiety, depression, or mental health concerns arise.

In this section, we will outline some risks you should be aware of when using medications that may be prescribed when a mother is mentally unwell during pregnancy.

The first group, we will cover are medicines that have risks of teratogenicity, that is congenital malformations that can happen during birth, and the second will look at medicine whose risks are linked to both withdrawal and toxicity.

Mood stabilizers, the first group we will cover, are a common way to combat depression, but they also come at a cost. Stabilizers have a small chance of deformation, as seen in teratogenicity. Anticonvulsants also have a risk of this deformation. This risk can be as high as a 17% when used in conjunction with sodium valproate, and up to 5% when used with all other types of compounds. Another stabilizer, lithium, can also cause some serious side effects. Lithium has a 0.05% absolute risk of cardiac malformation, and while this percentage is low, it is still something to keep in mind when using the substance.

In contrast to stabilizers, antidepressants have no consistent risk associated with them. There have been repeated findings of a smattering of different effects linked with SSRI's, but this has not been consistent with SNRI's. As such, there is not enough collected data to make a statement on this type of pill.

Antipsychotics are the last medication related to teratogenicity that we will discuss. Antipsychotics are another form of medication, but there is very little data regarding their side effects. However, from the data that has been collected regarding antipsychotics, clozapine has been shown to have a risk of serious side effects. As such, clozapine is measured as high risk. The data for this was minimal during the actual pregnancy process, but has shown signs of negative effects during breastfeeding.

When going over the above medications in terms of withdrawal and toxicity, there are also some effects that need to be considered as well. Lithium, when taken as a mood stabilizer, can cause newborns to be blue or even hypotonic (a state of very low muscle tone). Antidepressants, when studying their toxic effects, have a wide range of ailments that are commonly seen in approximately 30% of babies when their mothers use the pills. It should be noted that these effects worsen when venlaxafine is added to the mix.

Antidepressants also have a lot of side effects that pertain to unborn babies. Slight prematurity, including babies being small for their dates, are two of these effects. Antidepressants can also cause your baby to have difficulty breathing (respiratory problems), disturbance of sleep, as well as an increased risk of time in neonatal extensive care. When using antipsychotics, the effects on your baby are two fold. You increase the risk of having larger babies, which can be damaging in the same way that having a smaller baby can, and they can lead to metabolic instability as well.

The above medications can also lead to both neurobehavioral risks as well as risks later in pregnancy. Most of the risks associated with neurobehavioral aspects tend to be related to early development. Mood stabilizers, more specifically sodium valproate, can adversely affect the IQ of a child, which can in turn stunt growth and early stage development. Antipsychotics on the other hand, show a chance of delayed development, but this is still being investigated due to the small amount of evidence available. When looked at for neurobehavioral effects, antidepressants can increase development delays. This is usually confined to motor delays, and is associated with SSRI's. Antidepressants can also be linked to early autism. This link could be genetically based, but results have shown that children who experience autism with mothers that have been on antidepressants have seen a 2-fold increase in rates.

Antidepressants can also cause effects during your second and third trimesters. The first of these is persistent pulmonary hypertension in your newborn, which can lead to breathing problems. The other negative repercussion can be pregnancy hypertension, which refers to an increase in blood pressure that can be harmful to both you and your baby.

Benzodiazepines is the last form of medication we will cover for side effects. This type of treatment is generally prescribed to people who either suffer from anxiety or who have anxiety disorders. While older data suggests a correlation between benzodiazepines and cleft lip, there is very little data to back this claim. Women exposed to benzodiazepines during their first trimester are only at risk of genetic anomaly around 1% of the time. This medicine can also be related to prenatal syndrome, which can cause such maladies as feeding problems, hypothermia, and deficiency in the baby's muscle tone. Benzodiazepines have also been linked to numerous other complications, such as low Apgar scores, breathing difficulties, floppy muscles, unstable body temperature, alteration in heart rate, altered EEG measurement and malformation. There is no real data on the reproductive safety of other, non.-benzodiazepine anxiolytic and hypnotic agents. As such, their use during the pregnancy period is not recommended.

The facts listed above are not saying that medicine should not be used during your pregnancy, or even that it should be avoided. Rather, you should always be aware of what exactly you are putting into your body. Everything you do during pregnancy will have some effect on your birth in one way or another. Always be aware of side effects, but make sure to discuss your treatment with your health care provider since untreated or inadequately treated mental distress could pose an even greater risk to you and your pregnancy.

Sources: *Buist et al., Australian Family Physician. 2014; 43:182*

Campagne et al., Eur J Obstet Gynecol Reprod Biol. 2007; 135:145

10. Music Therapy

Beyond aromatherapy, there are numerous other types of medical practices that can be very beneficial as alternative uses to traditional medicine. One of these is music therapy, which has many positive effects that can help you during your pregnancy. Just as with aromatherapy, this is a great method for anyone who wants to try alternative help methods, or if the methods you are currently using aren't as successful as you would like. So, the most important question is, why use music as a form of therapy? Music has been used for its healing properties for hundreds of years all across different civilizations. The use of music in this way dates as back as far as the Greeks and Egyptians, but has a history of being used on almost every continent. These countless years have shown music's effect as a healant, and reveal why it is so effective when used as a form of therapy.

When used as a therapeutic method, music works best as a form of relaxation. This is because music has been shown to be able to neutralize negative emotions, which helps it push back on building distress. By neutralizing these emotions, it has the ability to raise your stress threshold, which makes dealing with stress much easier. In a similar vein, it also enables you to harmonize your inner processes. This can aid relaxation, and help you gain a better level of inner peace. Remember, gaining a better connection between body and mind is one of the key steps to cutting down on high levels of distress.

Music therapy, while having many mood-altering capabilities, is also beneficial in its ability to stimulate imagination. This may seem like a small factor compared to other benefits, but this stimulation often centers around the parts of the brain where feelings and emotions are transmitted. Music also triggers these same reactions in autonomic responses. These reactions can then lead to an overall better mood, and give you the ability to think and react more clearly. Both avenues are very important when it comes to keeping a strong mental focus, and reveal how to use music to its full capabilities.

Listening to good music causes a pleasure response from your brain. This response, as all good responses do, then causes a rush of endorphins, which serve as pleasure inducing chemicals. These endorphins are beneficial for two reasons. One, an increase in pleasure helps reduce distress by curbing anxiety and naturally relieving stress. Two, the releasing of endorphin causes a natural reaction to occur in which the concentration of the stress hormone in the blood is greatly diminished. This reduction also works to relieve stress, and shows the importance of stimulating endorphin release during pregnancy.

In addition to the above effects, people who listen to music as a form of healing have been shown to strengthen their body. Physicality from music comes from a couple of different factors. Such things include a lowering of your blood pressure and creating a healthy heart rate. It has even been shown to improve your overall respiratory rate. As all of these actions are centered around a healthy body, they are important to the health of your growing baby, which should always be your first priority.

All of these effects are very important to explain the benefits that music therapy can have. Music has also been shown to be effective when pertaining specifically to pregnant women. When used exclusively during pregnancy, music therapy has been shown to relieve anxiety levels as well as mellow out the mother. This state of relaxation can be very beneficial to induce long term rest. Music can also be used during the actual birth, as a way to help curb some of the pain that comes from the process.

Sources: *Chang et al., Journal of Clinical Nursing. 2008; 17:2580*

11. General Exercise

There are many different methods that can be helpful to pregnant women. We have already covered exercise in a couple of different capacities, but this section will focus on it as a much broader aspect. Mind and body are the two different parts of yourself that, as stated before, you need to work on while harboring a baby. Each is important, and while there are certain ways to make sure they are both strong, nothing will aid your physical form more than the implementation of exercise. Exercises can be broken down into different categories, each with varying degrees of severity, and all of them should be considered when trying to make your pregnancy as healthy as possible.

Overall, exercise has been shown to work as a natural stress reducer. Just like with music therapy, exercise naturally releases endorphins into your body. This will have many positive effects on both your mood as well as brain functions. Endorphins are a natural way to feel better, which gives any endorphin-producing workout the same effect as many mood-altering medications. Even so, these effects also go beyond simply stress. Anxiety, or any other negative moods, can be mitigated through the use of exercise and, if done correctly, is one of the best ways to stay upbeat.

There are two main types of exercises that are available to pregnant women. Each of these are great ways to help your body without causing harm to your baby. These two types are water and land exercises. When compared, each type has its own pros and benefits in conducing a successful pregnancy. Look at both and decide which one works the best for you.

Water exercises, which are the more favorable option to use during pregnancy, are centered around getting the workout you need in a pool. Typically, these are better for pregnant women because the water reduces the stress that exercise can put on your body. Working out on a hard surface, such as concrete or hardwood, can cause ailments like swollen feet or aching joints. Working out in water eliminates this. By reducing pain, your workout then becomes much more enjoyable, and, if the your workout is more enjoyable, you are more likely to keep up with your routine. Pools are also great spots to work out in due to your fluctuating figure. Just with Tai Chi, you want to take certain precautions as your baby continues to grow. You may not be as comfortable moving as you once were, and your body may seem foreign at time. While this may make running or ground exercises more difficult, working out in the fluidity of a pool can offset this.

Another benefit of water exercises is that working out in water makes falling or tripping almost impossible. This in turn makes your workout a safer process. Also, being submerged in water is easier on bodily harm because you no longer have to support your weight yourself. The water will help you evenly distribute your the added weight from your pregnancy, which can be a very welcome reprieve.

Your back, which is constantly under stress during pregnancy, and your legs, which also can come under stress due to the added baby weight, are also both more at ease because of this process. The water is a great way to both workout without pain and make sure that you suffer as little as possible. There are a plethora of different water-based exercises available to pregnant women, with light swimming being the most common. Swimming, or even wading, is a great, easy way to stay active. Water aerobics, is another light, water workout that can keep you in shape without giving you too much trouble. These are especially true later in pregnancy during the third trimester where you are at your largest size.

However, if you do not have the means, or the desire, to work out in water, working out on land can also be fine as long as you are careful. Here, you have to be take extra precautions, and be much more aware of your growing body. Any type of balance practice, be it yoga or some form of home workout, should usually be used in conjunction with these exercises, especially as you start to move further into pregnancy.

Any type of exercise you do during your pregnancy, no matter what stage, should always be light and low-impact. Light exercise is defined as any type of exercise that requires a little amount of effort. Keep in mind, when not in the water your joints and muscles will experience the full impact of whatever workout you choose to do. Jogging is a good way to keep in shape that will do your body very little harm, as will going for a walk. Stationary biking is even better, as it will allow you to work up a sweat, but will do so without the pounding or repetitive motion that running has. Just make sure your personal workout gives you positive effects, and it is as comfortable as possible. You never want to push yourself too far, and as you move into your nine months, just be aware that your body is constantly changing. Adapt to this change, keep it light, and you should be fine.

12. Acupuncture

Although it may sound jarring at first, acupuncture is a very successful way to treat the distress that comes during pregnancy. Many people may be wary of the prospect, which is understandable. However, as a form of relief, acupuncture dates back almost two thousand years. Today, it is used in many different situations for treating all sorts of pain, and its benefits have been proven useful for many different ailments. Here, we will discuss how it can be best used for pregnancy.

The positive effects of acupuncture have a wide range of benefits. Most of these benefits are centered around pain treatment, where it is most commonly used, but it also has many effects that go far beyond that. One of the most common uses for acupuncture, both in and outside of pregnancy, is for dealing with nausea. Nausea is a very common symptom that almost every pregnant woman exhibits in one way or another. It can occur during the start, middle and end of pregnancy, and be very, very uncomfortable. Acupuncture helps fight this in all stages, and is a method that can used in addition to medication or if your medication isn't giving you the desired results. You can use this method regardless of what type of nausea you are experiencing, be it morning sickness or simply general nausea.

Acupuncture has been shown to help with all sorts of problems that constantly plague pregnant women. This includes hip and back pain, breech position, labor induction as well as depression, both severe and mild. It may also help with sleep problems, and help with lasting fatigue. Each of these ailments, while they may not all apply to your pregnancy, can be dealt with if needed. This wide variety of solutions is why acupuncture can be so useful as a way to increase your overall health. This can especially useful if there is a certain type of ailment that you can't seem to break.

One of the largest and most comprehensive studies done on acupuncture during pregnancy was conducted during 2007 *(Bosco et al., Acupunct Med. 2007; 25:65)*. In this study, researchers found that acupuncture helped with a number of the distress problems we have covered in this guide. The main problem that was treated was irritability, which is linked to anger, anxiety as well as depression. The data suggests that acupuncture has the ability to treat each of these different emotional stresses, and can be very useful to pregnant women who feel under distress. As it helped with so many of these different problems, acupuncture also greatly improved the overall quality of life for women who took part in the study.

The above situations show why acupuncture can be a great way to help yourself through pregnancy. If you find that acupuncture is right for you, always remember to try and remember to find a qualified acupuncturist. This will ensure you will be as safe as possible during the process. Just as with any type of treatment, you want to find a person who has studied your treatment. Also, note that not all qualified acupuncturists specialize in dealing with pregnancy. Each acupuncturist may have been trained in different field.

You should try to find one that specifically deals with symptoms associated with pregnant women. If you can't find such a acupuncturist, then try and match up to one who knows how to treat some of the problems you are experiencing.

Beyond the needles, it is also understandable if you are worried about any side effects associated with acupuncture. However, these worries are largely unfounded. A 2002 study conducted at the Women's and Children's Hospital at Adelaid University in Australia, not only backed the positive effects of undergoing acupuncture during pregnancy, but showed that using the method had no visible side effects or negative repercussions. This data was discovered by running tests on women during their first trimester. This created the best environment, as it is the time where the fetus is the most vulnerable. The tests showed, after repeated results, that there were no visible side effects linked to the acupuncture process. In fact, this test has been repeated at many different universities across the globe, and none have shown that there is an increase of negative effects (such as stillbirth, miscarriages or premature birth) when acupuncture is used at any point in the pregnancy process. If you want to use acupuncture, you need not worry about it having any lasting effects on your or your child.

Sources: *Bosco et al., Acupunct Med. 2007; 25:65*

Smith et al., Birth. 2009; 36:246

13. Hypnotherapy

In a similar vein to acupuncture, another alternative method that can be used when trying to stop distress is hypnosis. Hypnosis is a word that may bring about a certain degree of suspicion, but it has been proven again and again to be a good tool when dealing with distress. Your mind is one of the most important factors when trying to make it through the pregnancy process, and hypnosis can greatly aid that. Instead of thinking of it as going under a spell, which will simply increase preexisting notions, you should think of hypnosis as a method that is used to put your mind into a better, more serene place.

In fact, when stripped down to its core, hypnosis is very similar to yoga in many ways. That may seem silly to say, but both methods have many commonalities. Hypnosis, like yoga, is mainly used as a form of relaxation, which of course reduces both stress and anxiety. If you have tried many methods of relaxation practices and had little success, hypnosis is a great process to turn to. The relaxation that comes from hypnosis can also help you in numerous other ways as well. Sleep, which can be a problem for some women, is greatly improved by this relaxation, as are general thoughts and ways of thinking. Wellness practices taught us the power of positive thinking, and hypnosis can eliminate both fears and worries associated with pregnancy, which enables a more positive attitude.

When seeking out hypnosis, there are two different methods you can use to induce the sleep. The first is using a trained hypnotist. Just like any other field, you want to make sure you are using a trained professional, which will allow you garner the best results from the process. However, if seeking out a hypnotists isn't right for you, there is also the option of self-hypnosis. Self-hypnosis is another good way to achieve a high level of relaxation without having to deal with any outside source.

Self-hypnosis is an odd form of hypnosis in that it requires no other person. As such, it can be very tricky to learn. However, when done right it works almost as a state of meditation (which will be covered in more detail below). Before starting out with self-hypnosis, be aware that such a state can only be achieved by high levels of practice and dedication. The more you work at, the easier it will be. In order to learn, self-hypnosis is usually achieved through the use of audio tapes. While it does work, many researchers have found that it is usually found to be less effective than working with someone else.

Even so, self-hypnosis can be a very effective way to ease the birthing process and labor. These benefits are why, if you wish to use this type of hypnosis, it is generally recommended you start in late in the second trimester. You then continue practicing it all the way through the birth, using the audio tapes to guide you. Repeating this process is essential during this time, as the repetition allows it to become habitual. Once the hypnosis is habitual, the entire process becomes easier, and will allow you to become more responsive to this type of therapy.

In order to further explore the effects of hypnosis, there are two studies that you should know about. The first of these took place during in 2009 (*Alexander, B., Turnbull, D., & Cyna, A. (2009). The effect of pregnancy on hypnotizability. American Journal of Clinical Hypnosis*).This study is important in that it didn't just look at the different effects of hypnosis, but it also examined how exactly hypnosis affected pregnant women overall. The findings of this study were quite informative. Researchers conducting the report found that, as a result of the tests, hypnosis was not only effective to women undergoing pregnancy, but exactly *why* hypnosis was so effective to women undergoing pregnancy. It turns out that, according to the date, women as a gender are much more susceptible to hypnosis while pregnant that when not. This allows the hypnosis to take much better that it normally would, and is the primary reason it can be used so effectively. The success also makes pregnant women much more open to the benefits of the process as well.

The second study whose data we will cite (*Beebe et al., Nurs Womens Health. 2014; 18:48*) was a recent one. This analyzed the effect the use of negative words in medical care can have on both the labor and pregnancy process. Words have a lot of power when it comes to our mind sets, and negative words that are used during the medical process can both magnify and intensify the amount of pain reporting. That is to say, the amount of pain being felt can be magnified due to the amount of negative language being used. As such, hypnosis, which reinforces the use of positive thinking, can actually decrease both anxiety and fear about pregnancy by cutting back on these negative terms.

Hypnosis has even proven to be effective during childbirth as a way to make labor easier. However, there are no concrete numbers in regards to this particular finding. It seems that, despite the positive effects that have been recorded from numerous studies, most women do not use hypnosis as a way to cope with pregnancy. This may be mainly due to the lack of information or awareness regarding hypnosis. That being said, hypnosis does have some minor adverse effects that are worth being aware of when deciding to implement this process. These side effects are mainly short lived bouts of pain, such as headaches or amnesia, but they usually go away naturally after a short duration of time. Hypnosis has proven useful for many different areas of life, helping people overcome all sorts of obstacles, and it can be very beneficial to the problems associated with pregnancy as well.

Sources: *Alexander, B., Turnbull, D., & Cyna, A. (2009). The effect of pregnancy on hypnotizability. American Journal of Clinical Hypnosis.*

Beebe et al., Nurs Womens Health. 2014; 18:48

14. Meditation

The next form of alternative treatment, meditation, is a useful way to relieve stress and anxiety through a controlled form of relaxation. In this guide, we have covered time and time again how important relaxation is at diffusing distress. Women who find they are more relaxed suffer less distress than those who aren't. Because of this, any form of therapy you are going to use centers around the idea of relaxation. Meditation is one of those ways that uses non-invasive methods to help achieve that process.

Meditation is a mental process that helps you by giving you a space and time to find some much needed relaxation. However, it also provides you with many physical benefits as well. These physical benefits work in conjunction with the mental relaxation to help you reduce distress, while giving you a healthier body. One of the most advantageous elements to meditation as a form of therapy is how safe it is. Meditation adds no stress on your body, avoids medicinal practices (which can have side effects) and, best of all, is quite easy to perform.

In the same vein as traditional exercise, meditation is beneficial in that it produces endorphins when performed. These endorphins improve your overall mood, and can leave you feeling good. In addition, meditation also reduces stress hormones. The reduction of these hormones greatly increase pain tolerance. An increased tolerance can come in handy for many pregnancy ailments you will experience such as joint pain or headaches. A higher pain tolerance also helps you endure labor much more easily than you normally would. Overall, a high pain tolerance will make the entire nine months go a lot more smoothly.

When studied, people who practice meditation have also been shown to have higher levels of both serotonin and melatonin in their body. Serotonin is a chemical compound linked to happiness, which helps improve moods and cut back on both anxiety and depression. Melatonin on the other hand, is a similar chemical compound that can help both induce and create a better sleep, which can be hard to come by as you progress through pregnancy. Melatonin is also beneficial because it can counteract the effects of acute stress, which can be dangerous as it commonly occurs with the immunosuppressive effect. An immunosuppressive effect refers to a reduction of the immune system, which can lead to an increase in infection. Meditation helps reduce this risk.

Meditation can be used all throughout your pregnancy, but it is especially helpful during the earlier stages when your body is going through its first changes. This is because meditation can offset many problems you will see in the first months, such as heartburn, nausea and constipation. Meditation also helps boost your energy, and greatly helps with fatigue. Both of these are in short supply at the beginning of the first trimester. Here, your body is working very hard to get your baby growing, which saps more energy and makes you more tired. Meditation can be very important to this growing process, by allowing you more energy that you would normally have.

When meditating, it can also be a good idea to listen to soft or relaxing music. This will help your child grow in a more relaxed environment. Meditation starts as a process built around helping your changing body, but gradually becomes more about mental health as the time moves on. While in your first trimester it can be good practice for physical ailments, during the second or third it becomes a great way to handle increased levels of stress or anxiety.

Something that should not be forgotten is, meditation is as physical as it is mental. Practicing meditation can have many similar effects to yoga, such as relaxing the spine. Relaxing your spine helps you maintain a better posture and takes stress off other parts of your body. Even toward the very end, when anxiety levels have been show to rise, it is a great tool to help you clear your mind, and stay positive while still moving forward. In this way, it is one of the best, cleanest forms of coping available to you throughout your entire term.

Sources: *Solberg et al., Med Sci Monit. 2004; 10:CR96*

15. Autogenics

Continuing on the trend of linking your mind and body as a way to control distress, Autogenic Therapy will be the next topic we discuss. Autogenic Therapy (or AT) is a natural build in to both yoga and meditation. This is because Autogenic Therapy, which was first developed during the later stages of the 1980's, is built around strengthening your overall self by serving you both mentally and physically. This balance is what AT is built off of, and the reason in can be so valuable to pregnant women.

At its base, Autogenic Therapy is a method used to influence one's autonomic nervous system, and help them achieve a natural level of relaxation. However, these exercises and practices do not simply create a stronger self, but they also help by giving you more self awareness. So, how exactly does this process work? And why it is so effective?

Unlike most distress reduction practices, AT is actually split into two distinct parts. Each of these is as important as the other to achieving the balance necessary to make the practice worthwhile. The first of these parts is physical, where one will partake in a small exercise that lasts around fifteen or so minutes a day. The second is mental. Here, the person working on said exercise will actually try to incorporate visualization into this process. This visualization is used to strengthen their mind while you are physically strengthening your body.

In relation to pregnancy, AT has been used in all three stages: the antenatal period, labor and post-natally. In each of these time frames, it has been used to treat such conditions as primary infertility, and has even helped with the birthing process. During the antenatal period, AT has been shown to reduce many common complaints. These range from breathlessness and nausea, to constipation and irritability. Anger and tension have also been shown to become greatly reduced in patients using Autogenic Therapy. Fear, which occurs in both forms of anxiety and stress, can also become normalized through this process. AT even helps prevent toxemia, which is a sharp rise in blood pressure during pregnancy. This occurs because AT commonly normalizes both blood pressure and heart rate while also reducing stress.

The next stage of pregnancy, labor, is aided by AT in a very similar manner as the antenatal period. Labor pain, one of the most daunting things about the entire birthing process, can be lessened by the use of autogenics. This is because Autogenic Therapy tends to create a sense of relaxation which, as covered in the section above, creates a natural tolerance to pain. This increase of tolerance allows the body to perform very well on its own. The added relaxation from this process can also reduce fear, and make it so breathing and heart rate stabilize at normal, healthy levels. When your heart rate is down, so are your risks for both stress and irritability.

In addition to labor, AT also helps the birthing process through other means. When used during pregnancy, it is shown the Autogenic Therapy has the ability to reduce cervical dilation by three to four hours. It can also increase the strength and effectiveness of contractions, while lowering their rate to one fifth. This makes the entire labor process one third shorter than normal, which means the birth becomes both quicker and easier than it would be without the implementation of AT. If this exercise is used in conjunction with the contractions and labor processes, then it can have great results at bringing about a large amount of pain relief.

The third and final period of birth, post-natal, can also be improved by use of proper therapy practices. Here, autogenics can help you recover from different psychological and physical effects that you may have undergone during labor. Nobody said having a child was easy, and labor can be particularly taxing both mentally and physically. However, Autogenic Therapy may either reduce the stress associated with labor, or make it much easier to deal with. AT has also been shown to cause boosts in milk production, and cut down on post-natal depression. If you suffer from insomnia, this method can also be used to help you get back to sleep on a regular basis. It also helps you return to sleep after night feeds.

A study at the Department of Obstetrics at the University of Warzburg looked at AT's effects on helping 1,000 mothers through labor. The data showed very convincing advantages of using AT over no treatment for the reduction and length of labor pain. Mother who trained in AT showed a 30% shorter labor, 20% fewer contractions and a much easier birthing experience. A similar study, also carried out of the University of Warzburg, showed that, of 302 women who had used

Autogenic Therapy during pregnancy, 70% of them experienced significant pain relief. These results show just how effective AT can be as a pain reducer.

16. Biofeedback Therapy

The next step in our journey to help reduce distress comes in the form of biofeedback. Biofeedback, as its name might suggest, is the act of seeking relief through the use of electronic devices. These devices are used to allow patients (pregnant women) the ability to control, or at least give some regulation to, certain body functions that are not normally under their control. In this, the devices help with the physical processes. By controlling these processes, women have a better, easier time during their pregnancy.

Biofeedback is typically used by women who want to try and cure their depression without having to deal with the side effects that medication can bring. In a study conducted at UNC Hospitals Prenatal Inpatient Psychiatry Unit (PPIU) from January 31, 2012 – June 1, 2012, researchers studied the overall effects of biofeedback using a form of therapy called heart rate variability biofeedback (HRVB). This therapy, which helps regulate a normal heartbeat, has shown to cure many different ailments, including prenatal depression as well as anxiety. This process works by allowing patients the ability to recognize and interpret the signals of their own heartbeat, which they can use to better their overall health.

HRVB helps control heart rate variability (HRV) which is a common factor in causing both depression and anxiety. As such, women who use HRVB during the pregnancy have a better chance at stopping anxiety, which has been linked to postnatal depression among other harmful pregnancy effects. Using this feedback helps fight depression by cutting it off at the source, which prevents it from building into a larger problem.

In this study, pregnant women over the age of 18 were taken to a room where they individually participated in two distinct 30 minute to 1 hour sessions of HRVB. The first of these sessions was in place to help teach the women about their own biofeedback, while the second session was for them to actually use and implement what they had learned. Here, they used deep, abdominal or diaphragmatic breathing techniques to

disengage from anxious and/or stressful thoughts and emotions. They then put these methods into practice and were showed how to use them after leaving the hospital.

The results of the study concluded that women who were correctly using and adapting the different HRVB techniques actually saw a noticeable increase in physiological coherence. They had a sounder mind, and their overall mentality improved. While HRVB has many benefits, the study concluded it was most effective at battling acute anxiety as well as the symptoms associated with prenatal depression. In fact, women who suffered from postpartum depression were more likely to show anxious features compared with depressed women not in the postpartum period. As such, heart rate variability biofeedback has shown to be extremely effective at combating this depression both with inpatients as well as outpatients.

It should be noted that there was no control used in this study, which does make the data somewhat weaker overall. Still, the results of this biofeedback have been shown through many different tests. As a technique, biofeedback is very beneficial to anyone who is suffering from depression, but it is particularly helpful to women who are undergoing pregnancy. There is always the option of using antidepressants to treat pregnancy related depression, but these have so many side effects, many try to avoid them. If you are one of those people, biofeedback can be a great way to keep your mind sound. Even in outpatients, research has shown that repeated use of biofeedback after discharge from the hospital can have long term lasting effects.

Using heart rate variability biofeedback has also been associated with statistically significant improvement on all instrument scores. The greatest of these have been STAI (State Trait Anxiety Inventory) scores. This reinforces the positive aspects of biofeedback, and reveal how supportive it can be as a way to cope with problems. There are exercises that help your mind and some that help your body, but none work as well to help both together quite like biofeedback therapy.

Sources: *Beckham et al., Arch Womens Ment Health. 2013; 16:59*

17. Dance

While we covered many forms of exercise in the earlier section, one type that we did not cover is dancing. Dancing is a good, fun way to get exercise that also allows you to workout in a safe way. There are several types of dancing available to pregnant women, and each one has different physiological benefits.

Typically, just as with exercise, you want to dance in a way that puts the least amount of stress on your body. This will ensure you can get a workout while also keeping you and your baby safe as safe as possible. When looking to dance, if you don't have options at your local gym, you can also try to seek out an independent studio or classes to find a session that will be best for you. However, even if you do not have access to a class, you can still dance in your own living room. Movement more than method is the key. Typically, it is best to dance around three to four times a week in separate, thirty minute sections. As an added caution, you can even combine dancing with other forms of exercise, such as swimming and yoga, to make sure that you put the least amount of stress on your muscles and joints.

The first, and most important, thing about incorporating dancing into your weekly routine is making sure you find the right type of session for you. While dancing on your own is still a good type of exercise, be aware there are plenty of options if one doesn't fit you right. Just make sure, whichever one you choose, that your instructor knows that you are pregnant, which will help them accommodate you.

During the first trimester, jazz, samba, ballroom dancing (no lifts) and salsa can all be ideal ways to keep you fit. As time moves on, these dances may be harder to do. As a result, you might want to switch to something that is a little easier. Belly dancing, which we will cover soon, is the best way to go during the later stages. Remember, all forms of exercise should be kept light, and dancing is no different. Low-impact dancing that requires little jumping or repeated jerky movements is one of the best ways to make sure your dancing habits are as safe as possible. For this, you want to keep to any type of dancing that keeps one foot on the floor at all times. Hip hop and urban street dances should be avoided, as they require a lot of jerky or sudden movements. Tap dancing should be avoided for the same reason, and you should also only attempt ballet if you are already familiar with the craft. Now is not the time to branch out to unknown territory.

These rules may seem tricky, but if you listen to your body and are aware of the signs that happen you are overdoing it, you should be fine. The golden rule is to always resist stress on your body, which means avoiding anything too rigorous. If you ever experience light headedness, or any shortness of breath, it is always a good idea to sit down and allow yourself to recover before moving forward.

During the first trimester you can dance just as you would normally as long as you take good precautions. The most important things to remember here are, always warm up before you start, and make sure you have water handy. You never want to become dehydrated, nor do you want to risk injury by not having properly stretched limbs. It is also a good idea to dance in a place that is open or well ventilated. Overheating can be a serious problem, but it can be avoided if you dance in a space that is kept cool.

As you move into the later stages of pregnancy, when the aforementioned types of dancing become too difficult to perform, belly dancing is one of the best, safest options available to you. Belly dancing is a great workout, that helps strengthen both your core and belly muscles. These muscles are good to grow as they help lessen stress on your back, and work to give you better posture. When performing belly dancing, which is also a low-impact form of exercise, you are also working your pelvic floor muscles. These are notable as, when strengthened, they can help you not leak when sneezing or coughing.

One of the largest benefits of belly dancing is the help it will give you during both labor and the birthing process. Belly dancing strengthens your lower core muscles that are commonly used during labor, which will help you reduce pain during birth. This style of dancing also helps, as stated, the pelvic floor muscles, which are also very key during birth. Vaginal muscles are also used during belly dancing. Strong vaginal muscles can set a good base of the bladder and uterus, which makes pushing during labor much easier and eases the process overall.

In the ways mentioned above, dancing can be easily implemented during the birthing process to reduce pain. Birth requires a large amount of different muscles to push your baby out into the world. Belly dancing, as it is centralized at your core where your baby is held, helps all of these muscles grow. Even your leg muscles, such as quadriceps, are made stronger through belly dancing. Strong legs help you move, which gives better support to your body.

Dancing is a great way for pregnant women to strengthen their body, and maintain strength as they grow. However, dancing is not recommended to every women going through pregnancy. If you have complications, are suffering from back pain, or have problems with your pelvis, you should consult a physician before attempting any dancing, regardless of type. However, if you are having a successful pregnancy, this is one of the best low-impact ways to make sure you maintain the strong level of fitness you need. Just be aware of what stage you are in, and stick to the styles that are best for that period.

Sources: *Abdolahian et al., Global Journal of Health Science. 2014; 6:219*

18. Progressive Muscle Relaxation and Guided Imagery

The next two techniques are extremely effective at garnering both physical and physiological benefits. These are guided imagery and progressive muscle relaxation. Each of these has a smattering of benefits that can be very important throughout all the different stages of pregnancy.

We will first look at how progressive muscle relaxation (PMR) can help you during this process. Progressive muscle relaxation is a physical therapy technique that is aimed at helping with back pain, one of the most common adverse effects of long-term pregnancy. Back problems can have negative effects on all parts of your body, such as knees and legs. As such, you want to do everything in your power to avoid putting extra stress or tension on your back and spine. PMR is one of the best ways to help you do just that.

The technique of PMR involves using deep breathing in conjunction with muscle tension followed by relaxation to facilitate progressive relaxation of major muscles. Here, that same method is used on the muscles that support your back, which can help alleviate pain. Beyond these contractions, muscle relaxation is a very important part of PMR as well. Muscle relaxation is important as another great form of reducing stress on your body. Independently, these muscle exercises are very good for your health, but are ever more beneficial when combined with deep, heavy breathing. This combination results in positive benefits, all of which will help your back support, muscle relaxation and allow you better control over your body as your baby continues to grow.

PMR helps with back problems, but it especially centralizes with lower back pain. This is because the prevalence of lower back pain in pregnancy, with 50 to 70 percent of pregnant women experiencing one form or another. It was described as severe in 25% of pregnant women, moderate in 30%, and mild in 45.6%. The average prevalence of pain was 56.7%. More than 80% of pregnant women with back pain experience discomfort during daily activities, and have difficulties with housework, child care, and job performance. In addition, the added weight of the fetus, combined with the natural added weight that comes with pregnancy, can have many negative effects, such as destabilizing the spine and sacroiliac joints. These numbers and effects reveal the importance of dealing with this pain. PMR is one of the best, and most widely used ways to do so.

The effects of progressive muscle relaxation were recorded in a study (*Akmese et al., Journal of Midwifery and Women's Health. 2014; p:503*) where 66 pregnant women were monitored for the effects that PMR had on their pregnancy. The women used were not undergoing any other complementary therapy, but rather just focused on using PMR to treat their back pain. Through the study, the women who were not administered PMR (control group) saw an increase in back pain over the eight weeks, while the women who underwent PMR (experimental group) saw a reduction to their pain. In every scale, there was a noticeable difference between the experimental and the control group. Those results reveal the effectiveness of PMR when used for this process. At the baseline, women who underwent PMR also had a much higher level of mental health, which will be covered in more detail below.

Controlling the muscular tension in your body is an acquired skill that can also bring about some great mental benefits. Though the focus of PMR is on relaxing the muscles of the body, there is also a psychological benefit to using it as well. It is suggested that since the parasympathetic nervous system dominates during muscle relaxation, the practice of PMR may aid in reducing heart rate, blood pressure, and anxiety. Doing anything for a set amount of time, or working it into your daily routine, will allow you to create a pattern. The constant tensing and relaxing of your muscles is one example of this pattern. Such a pattern can bring about a state of peacefulness. This peacefulness brought on by progressive muscle relaxation has then been shown to help lower anxiety. In addition, parasympathetic dominance can also help create this state as well.

The other type of meditation we will look at in this section, to once again connect to the overarching theme of linking your mind and body, is guided imagery through visualization techniques. Guided imagery is a way to enter a relaxed state through outside aid. This visualization helps you become relaxed, and can be thought as a similar form of meditation. However, guided imagery differs as it solely focuses on the connection that your mind and body have. Every thought that you have, due to this connection, will have a physical response associated with it. In this way, guided imagery has been shown to be very effective when used in conjunction with PMR. Guided imagery, when looked at as an overall health benefit, has many positive effects on different parts of your body. Each of these can be very important in maintaining a good health, such as lowering heart rate and reducing cardiovascular activity.

When practicing PMR, or incorporating it into your active therapy, make sure to combine it with guided imagery. When practicing any type of therapy throughout your pregnancy, you want to make sure to work on as much as yourself as possible. The positive effects of having a healthy physical and mental behavior have been shown many times through this guide. As such, although working on each of these methods individually is very good, if you have a chance to combine any of them, such as the case with PMR and guided imagery, try to do so.

Sources: *Akmese et al., Journal of Midwifery and Women's Health. 2014; p:503*

Urech et al., Psychoneuroendocrinology. 2010; 35:1348

Jallo et al., Evidence-based Complementary and Alternative Medicine. 2014; 2014:1

19. Reading and Writing

This next section will once again reiterate perhaps one of the most important aspects of reducing stress and creating a healthy, successful pregnancy: keeping a positive attitude. The psychological effects of negativity have been proven by scientists again and again, and these harmful effects can seep into all different areas of your life. This can become even more extrapolated by the natural stress that comes during pregnancy. Such thoughts can lead to depression, which should be a concern for any pregnant woman. Bad thoughts and negativity can be detrimental to every aspect of pregnancy. Here, we will explain one unconventional tool you can use to try and cope with or conquer these bad thoughts: writing.

While you may not think it, writing can be a very useful method to helping you battle depression throughout your pregnancy. Self-awareness is very important to maintaining a strong mind, and writing can help create a higher level of self-awareness. This is done in two steps. One, identifying the problem at hand, and two, then realizing why that problem is not as big or daunting as it may first seem. This type of thought process will allow you to better understand and face your problems. When trying to face your problems in this way, it is often best to go about this through keeping a diary or personal notes.

When you are faced with a problem during pregnancy (and you most likely will be) it is often a good idea to write that problem down. Once you do, you can then write yourself a note explaining why there is no real reason to worry about said problem. This mimics the process explained above, but the act of actually writing it down is an important distinction. This is because, the writing of a problem gives you something to refer back to should that problem rise again, which helps you move forward. Writing in this manner is a great way to cope with negative thinking, and can also be used to curb bad thoughts that may be reoccurring in your life.

Another way to use writing as a mental tool is through the use of a diary. Pregnancy is a process that is going to bring about a lot of changes in you both physically and mentally. Keeping a personal journal can be an effective way to sort out your feelings regarding these changes, which allows you to get a better sense of what's going on. Diaries can also help in organizing your worries, which act as a form of self-reflection, and can help bring any problems you have to light. A diary can even be more effective than a therapist at times, as it is not so constrained. When writing for yourself, there is no pressure, no other human that you need to think about. This then allows some extra clarity as well as a personal space to say exactly what you want in the exact way you want to say it. That freedom brings a more relaxed feeling to the process, and may help you discover some things that previously went unnoticed.

In addition to keeping a diary, or if you feel that you want to express yourself in a different medium, writing your story has also been found to be beneficial to the health of a pregnant woman. This style of autobiographical writing can also be very important when maintaining the relationships of those around you. This is because, going back and reflecting on some of the things you have talked about or said to others may make you more aware of your place in the world. It will also allow you to realize the connections you have with others in your life. The act of writing can serve as a therapeutic process, helping you find some peace and creating a certain level of relaxation.

If you do wish to try story telling, know that it can also be used in conjunction with another person. For instance, writing down your story, reflecting upon the important parts, understanding how they relate to what you are currently feeling, and then talking it over with a professional can be a great way to incorporate writing into normal therapy. When doing this, be aware of the power writing can have, and make sure to get someone you trust, be it a loved one or a professional, by your side during the process.

Writing will help you on many fronts, but is particularly strong at dealing with things that affect your mind. Bad thoughts, general negativity, depression and anxiety can all be helped through the use of pen and paper. There is a lot that happens throughout the course of a pregnancy, and in that time it is easy to get lost or forget yourself. Your mentality may become dark or sad at times, but always remember you are in control of your thoughts. Writing them down on paper, especially with tips and reminders from yourself on why things are never as bad as they seem, will help you never forget that.

20. Taking Supplements

By now, you have probably noticed that treating distress is no easy task. Combating your problems is something that takes time, dedication, hard work and pure determination. However, sometimes, those things are not enough, Sometimes, you have to turn to additional methods. One of those methods is the use of natural supplements, which will help boost your overall health as well as serve to fight off certain types of distress you might be struggling with.

As stated at the start of this guide, you and your baby are connected throughout childbirth. The healthier you are, the higher the chances that your baby is healthy. Using supplements as a way to make sure you have all the vital nutrients and vitamins for both you and your baby can be a very good idea. Vitamins have many different benefits that can help with both physical as well as mental issues. Knowing which ones to take can be as important as actually taking them, as that will give you the best desired effect.

Each supplement you choose to take will be administered for a certain purpose. Those purposes can range from small effects to much larger ones. For instance, if you are having problems with anxiety, it may be best to try and use supplements that are known to reduce anxiety, such as Vitamin D or Zinc. B12, another good supplement, helps strengthen your immune system, which is very important during pregnancy. It also helps deal with anxiety, as it is known to have natural calming effects. B12 also, while not a cure, can also be utilized as a way to lessen or ease signs of depression.

Another beneficial supplement you have available to you are omega-3 fatty acids. These fatty acids have many different benefits related to pregnancy regarding both you and your baby. Women who were studied to have high numbers of omega-3 fatty acids in their diet typically gave birth to strong, more advanced children. The children whose mothers had a large amount of the omega-3 fatty acid docosahexaenoic acid (DHA) have been shown to have much more advanced attention spans in their early life than those whose mothers did not. In fact, these babies typically showed these signs far into their second year of life, and their attention levels were almost two months ahead of babies whose mothers did not have high levels of the acid.

DHA may also be central to early brain development, which is yet another benefit to using this supplement. Attention is a very important factor is building early intelligence, and DHA comprises a large amount of an infant's brain during the first two years. As such, it makes sense that women who have a lot of DHA are more prone to give birth to children who develop intelligence a lot quicker than those born to mothers who have lower levels. The effect of DHA on the brain is not fully known. However, it is known that it is concentrated much more heavily in the brain and spine than anywhere else in the body, suggesting it is important to the growing of those areas. The advantages of high levels of DHA in the mother have been shown to last for some time, which can be very essential to the way a child develops.

You want to be as healthy as possible during pregnancy, and this can become difficult as time moves on. Aside from the above supplements, there are other good vitamins that can help you during your impregnation. Both depression and anxiety are lasting modes of distress that can occur often during the nine month period. However, there are a number of vitamins that can fight back against both of these well known ailments.

Vitamin D, which can be easily taken in pill form, is a great supplement that has been shown to boost both brain development and function in children. It also serves as a natural stimulant to the production of serotonin, a natural chemical that stimulates positive feelings in our brain. This increase in serotonin is one of the foremost ways to combat depression. However, depression can also be combated with zinc, B12 and omega-3's. Low levels of all of these nutrients have been linked to depression, so making sure you have normal levels will offset that. Plant phytochemicals can also be used to battle depression as well. These can be takes in supplement form, but also naturally occur in some type of foods. Probiotic supplements are another good way to treat depression. In fact, this is how certain medicines treat it as well.

Medicine can be very beneficial to people looking to treat some of their more serious pregnancy related problems. However, as the above information shows, supplements can also be very beneficial as a way to treat your problems in a more natural way. Where vitamins and nutrients have little to no side effects, medicine can. It is normal, especially when undergoing pregnancy, to want to try and mitigate these side effects as much as possible. Supplements are a great way to achieve this. These supplements can also be used alongside other forms of therapy, both mental and physical, which can enhance your health overall. Doing your own research, and learning about your own ailments, is very important to making sure you are taking the supplement that is right for you. Just remember, it is never a bad idea to get a second opinion from a professional before taking anything.

21. Massages

Your body is perhaps the most important aspect to a successful pregnancy. It connects to your mind and helps both support and feed your baby. If you take proper care of it, and manage to stay away from aches and pains, you will simply have an easier time overall. This is where the topic of this section, massages, comes into play.

Massage therapy is a great way to keep your body limber. In this way it has been shown to have numerous benefits to anyone who wants to reduce strain on their ligaments and joints. It also has many physiological benefits, which will be discussed shortly, and, as with all of the alternative methods in this guide, helps out your mind by creating a state of relaxation. Massages have been shown to create numerous benefits to pregnant women, and can be especially effective during labor.

You yourself might want to undergo the process of massage therapy during your pregnancy. This is, just as it sounds, using massages to relieve stress and tension in your body that can occur as you advance into the different trimesters. Massage therapy has been shown to have significant health benefits, including a reduction of stress and depression while also the lowering of both leg and back pain.

Pregnant women who underwent massage therapy have also been shown to have a drop in cortisol levels. This level drop is significant in that it lowers excessive fetal activity, as well as the rate of premature births. In terms of labor pain, women who have undergone massage therapy as a way to cope during childbirth have also seen many positive effects. The largest of these was a general reduction of labor induced pain, and an increase of vagal activity due to the stimulation of pressure receptors. On average, labor tended to be shorted by around three hours. These shortened labors also required less medication.

All of these above benefits were seen in a study published by NIH public access, published under *Expert Rev Obstet Gynecol*. 2010, March. Three studies were conducted in this write-up, and each one gave data to support the success that massage therapy can have. In the first of these studies, pregnant women were gives massage therapy by professional therapists 20 minutes a week over the course of five weeks. The second study had pregnant women being massaged by their significant others over a 16-week period. Each study showed the women to have a significant decrease in both depression and anxiety alongside their decrease in cortisol levels. Both studies, to further legitimize the benefits that massage therapy can have, also resulted in better pregnancy outcomes, such as a reduction in excessive fetal movement, which is more commonly seen in depressed women.

The third study used pregnant women who have been diagnosed with severe depression. These women were administered massage therapy twice a week over a 12 week period. This therapy gave them reduced levels of depression all throughout pregnancy, and these effects even lasted after birth.

Their newborns were also less likely to be born premature, and these massages resulted in less low birth weight. Postpartum depression was also reduced in women who underwent the massages, which shows the lasting effects of these benefits.

Prenatal complications have also been seen to reduce, as in the case of the study at hand, with use of massage therapy. Babies born to mother who used such therapies were generally healthier, due a large reduction in birth complications, and all types of depression, both during and after pregnancy, was largely reduced. This reduction in depression is very important, not only for the health of the mother, but this also makes the chance of bonding with an infant much higher after pregnancy occurs.

Massage therapy is also very beneficial in helping reduce stress hormone levels. As you can imagine, reducing these stress hormones leads to stress reduction. A drop in these levels has been shown to create stress reduction, which then increases positive pregnancy outcomes. These outcomes make the entire pregnancy process much smoother, and can range through any of the examples seen above; ranging from a reduced rate in prematurity to a reduction of overall labor pain.

In dealing with mental ailments, massage therapy has shown to increase cerebral flow in different brain regions involved in depression and stress regulation, such as the hypothalamus and amygdala. The increased vagal activity which occurs has also been linked to a reduction in both heart rate and blood pressure. Both of these events decrease anxiety through a state of relaxation.

Massage therapy, due to all of its potential benefits, is one of the most common forms of alternative treatment for pregnant women. It has been shown to be effective at treating pain, aches, depression, anxiety as well as birth complications. As long as they are performed on a weekly basis, these massages can be administered by either a professional or by your significant other. If you want a safe way to try and minimize the number of complications that can occur during both pregnancy and birth, massage therapy could be a great avenue to take.

Sources: *Field et al., Expert Rev Obstet Gynecol. 2010; 5:177*

22. Preparing for the Birth

As you move through your trimesters and learn to deal with the different types of distress you will encounter during your pregnancy, eventually you will have to start preparing for the most important part of the entire process: birth. Adequately preparing for the birth of your child can be a very exciting and important part of the entire process. In order to properly prepare, there are many different things you need to keep in mind. Each of these will be laid out below to make it easier for you to remember. Being properly prepared will make the birthing process astronomically easier. One of the best ways to do this is to make a checklist, which is a great way to keep things in order. This will allow to more easily organize the necessary things you need for the birth.

The largest, and most obvious, reason that a good birth preparation can be helpful is it will help put your mind at ease. Making a list, or knowing exactly what you need to do, will drop a lot of last-minute stress, which will save you a lot of anxiety that can occur from being unprepared. This section will both list and explain a certain number of different items that need to be kept in mind to make sure you are ready for the birth. This will make the entire process much less daunting, and help you relax your thoughts. Before we begin, note that, should you plan on having a caesarean (C section), you want to talk to your obstetrician about what might happen

Before your delivery, you want to make sure you have the list of necessary things in order as to make the process go more smoothly. First, you want to make sure when to go the hospital. That is, be aware of what symptoms are good markers that you birth is near. In that same vein, it is a good idea to be pre-registered at the hospital where you plan to give birth. This will allow you to get into a room much easier, as will knowing your preferences for both labor and delivery. You also want to be as familiar with the hospital you are going to give birth at as possible. Know how you want the birthing process to go, and then seek that outcome. This will give you the best mental state going into labor. Part of the preparation is knowing your care unit's day and night phone numbers, which will allow you stay in touch with them. You can also then call them should complications arise.

One of the most important aspects of going to the hospital is actually getting there. As such, it is best to always plan your transportation, as well as back up transportation in case something goes wrong. Know who is supposed to take you, and where they usually are. Additionally, also know what entrance at your hospital is best for you to take once you're there, as you are going to want to get inside as soon as you can. It will also be helpful if you know every entrance that can help you, which includes things such as emergency and after-hours entrances, just to make sure you will always have access to the quickest way inside. If you are donating your cord blood, makes sure to have those plans already made long before you go into the hospital.

Labor is a long, tiring process for any women. You want to have a large collection of different items available to you during this process that will make it so you can feel comfortable during your trip to the hospital. Medical information, which will make your checking in process much simpler, is one of these items. In addition, also make sure you have your socks, slipper and breast pads. These will give you a level of comfort. Chapstick, music and loose fitting clothes are all important for this exact same reason. A camera is great to have handy, which will allow you to capture the moment. Snacks for your significant other can be extremely important, as can the numbers of your friends and loved ones to make sure they don't miss the occasion.

After birth, you are going to want your baby to be as comfortable as possible. This can be done with many simple items, such as an infant sleeper (complete with legs) or a t-shirt. You will also want to make sure you have a diaper on hand for your baby to wear home.

Small toiletries, such as a toothbrush, comb and toothpaste could be beneficial for any children you already have, or can help anyone else who might need such items. It is always a good idea to have some things to make the drive home as comfortable as possible for your newborn. A baby blanket can be a good item that will help your baby keep warm during this time. An infant car seat, to make sure the trip is as safe as it can be, is also a great tool. Try to have one in your car to be ready when the time comes. If you already have children, getting them gifts "from the baby" can be a good idea to help them welcome their sibling into the world.

Once your baby is born, there is also a list of supplies you'll need to have ready. Though these can be purchased after the birth, it is a good idea to have them ready for before hand. The following list is comprised of items that will be essential for your newborn, and be central to the first years of your child's life.

When you baby first comes home, you want to be able to provide them with everything they need. These items, if gotten before pregnancy, will have you better prepared and reduce later stress. The first items on your checklist should be related to breastfeeding. If you are planning to breastfeed your baby, you want to have the proper supplies, such as nursing bras and pads. Even if you are not preparing to breastfeed, you should still have supplies such as nursing bottles and nipples on hand. If you aren't breastfeeding, you want to have some formula on hand as your substitute for milk.

Beyond breastfeeding, you want to have other preparations on hand to prepare for taking your newborn home. One of the most important of these are diapers and diaper related products. This includes a diaper pail, to throw away the dirty diapers, as well as diaper pins. It is also a good idea to keep a changing table, or a space where you can change your baby. Cotton balls, wash cloths, mild soap, diaper rash ointment, hair brushes and a thermometer are also essential to making this process as easy as possible.

Receiving blankets are another item that will help your newborn get the best sleep that they can. Make sure you have T-shirts and infant sleepers for this same reason. A sweater and cap will make sure your baby keeps warm. Make sure to have a place for your baby to sleep, be it a crib, cradle or bassinet. In connection with this, get both crib sheets and blankets. Your baby does not need a pillow to sleep on, so getting one is unnecessary, but you should get waterproof pads for the crib as well as for your lap. These are all the items you should have to be as ready as you can for your newborn to come home.

23. Sleep

Sleep is one of the most important elements to a peaceful, healthy pregnancy that we have not covered yet. The importance of sleep in relation to human health has been proven in many different tests throughout the years, and getting enough sound sleep is even more important during your pregnancy. Your health, both mental and physical, is extremely dependant on getting a good night's rest.

Even with all of the methods and practices we have covered, you may feel some stress during pregnancy. While this is natural, you want to make sure and listen to your body. One of the best ways to reduce stress during pregnancy is to always make sure you are getting enough sleep. Even if you are not exhibiting stress, if you are tired, go to bed. It will be much better in the long run for both you and your baby.

Sleep has been shown to be most important during the third trimester. Poor third-trimester subjunctive sleep has been linked as a risk factor to postpartum depression. Keeping a good schedule, and following some of the tips outlined in the following paragraphs will help stop this problem from occurring.

There are many different complications and elements of distress that can prevent you from getting a sound, good night's sleep. However, sleep is one of the best periods for your body to rest, which makes getting enough of it essential. These complications can range from health concerns such an increased heart rate, to something as simple as more trips to the bathroom. Pregnancy hormones can also increase during pregnancy, which may cause shortness of breath, and heartburn, in addition to natural aches and pains, can also occur. Both of these also cause sleep deprivation.

The first rule of sleeping during pregnancy is, do not use sleep aids or any herbal sleep medication. These have been shown to be harmful to pregnant women and can cause damage to your baby. In addition, also avoid any caffeinated drink such as soda, coffee or tea as they will cause you to stay up at night more regularly. Continuing with that thought, it is also best to avoid eating big meals or drinking a lot of liquid before bed. These habits can compromise your sleep cycle. Some women find it helpful to have a large breakfast and lunch, and then couple that with a small dinner.

If nausea is one of the main reasons you stay up at night, and it can be for certain women, crackers can help. Simply eat a few before bed and see if this helps stem the effects. Another important aspect to a good night of sleep is routine. A good routine can condition your body for bed, and allow you to fall asleep when the time comes. To achieve such a routine, try to go to bed, as well as wake up, the same time each day and night. This may seem hard to do at first, but with a little practice, you will have your set routine in no time.

Relaxation and prepping your body for sleeping are both important elements to a good night's rest. Each of these can be achieved by relaxing before bedtime. Relaxation can pertain to a number of activities, including taking a warm, 15 minute bath or drinking warm milk. However, anything you do that helps you relax will suffice. Relaxation before bed will make your body more ready for sleep, as well as help tire you out in the process. Exercise, though beneficial in many ways, is not recommended before bed. This is because exercise stimulates the body, releasing endorphins, which will make it hard to fall asleep in the same way drinking caffeine will.

Leg cramps can also be a concern for pregnant women, and they make it hard to keep sleeping through the night. There is not much you can do about preventing these cramps, as they tend to happen while you are asleep. However, once awake, you want to make sure these cramps go away as quickly as possible. To do this, press your feet hard against a wall or stand on the leg to reduce the cramping sensation.

Symptoms of anxiety or stress are also linked to restlessness, and can make it hard to stay asleep. These factors, as they are mental rather than physical, should both be prevented in the same way. A childbirth class, which can help you feel much more prepared for the future, is one way to try and calm down both symptoms to achieve the sleep that you are missing. Your doctor is also a great resource to have. If you are experiencing trouble sleeping due to distress, talk to him or her about what you can do to lessen these problems. Listen to your doctor, and work with them to figure out which solution may be best for you.

Being comfortable is also very important to getting some much needed rest. There are many ways to sleep, but some are specifically helpful in inducing a peaceful night. Sleeping on your side with your knees bent is one of these ways. This is due to the fact that this position takes your baby away from your veins, and allows better blood flow through your system. When doing this, it is recommended to sleep on your left side rather than you right. Laying on your left side can increase blood flow to the fetus, heart, uterus and kidneys while also taking stress off of your liver. You may switch to your right side if your left hip becomes sore, but you never want to lay flat on your back. A pillow between your legs can also enable you a better, more comfortable position in which to sleep.

The most important thing to remember when trying to set up a good sleep schedule is you always need to make sure you get a good amount of rest. This means, if you are finding it hard to sleep during the night, it may be best for you to take small naps throughout the day. This will make it easier to fall asleep at night, and also allow you to make up for lost sleep during the night.

Sources: *Wu et al., Med Sci Monit. 2014; 20:2740*

24. Healthy, Well-Scheduled Eating

As we move forward in discussing the best ways to stay healthy during pregnancy, it is impossible to ignore the benefits of a good diet, especially since diet has been suggested to have an impact on overall mood. Fluctuations in blood sugar can lead to mood and energy changes, deficiencies have been associated with symptoms such as depression, and too much caffeine is known to increase anxiety. There is an important relationship between the food we eat and our moods, making a balanced diet vital to a calm and healthy pregnancy. Just as with exercise, the benefits of eating healthy have already been proven, but these benefits are much more important when it comes to pregnant women. Keeping yourself healthy is not just central to a good pregnancy, but it is also important to making sure your baby gets the proper nutrients and vitamins they need. A good, balanced diet will help with this, and can even reduce building stress.

To properly evaluate and explain this section, we will first break down some foods that you should be eating. Then, we will expand that to include other foods, and mark which are best during each trimester. This will give you a clear idea of how to eat clean, and why those methods are so important.

Six foods that are very essential to a healthy pregnancy are whole grains, beans, salmon, eggs, berries and low-fat yogurt. Starting with the first, whole grains give you large amounts of both folic acid and iron, which are very good for the health of you and your baby. They also have more fiber than grains such as white rice and white bread. Whole grains consists of foods like whole-grain breads and cereals, and they can easily be incorporated into your average diet. You can have brown rice with dinner, use whole-grain bread for your sandwiches during lunch, and substitute your normal breakfast with oatmeal. Whole wheat pasta is another good, delicious source of whole grains.

Any type of beans, ranging from kidney to garbanzo to pinto, are an easy, nutritious incorporation into your diet. Beans can be put into salad, soups and chilis, and can even be incorporated into pasta dishes. Beans provide both protein and fiber, while also giving you access to a plethora of nutrients such as iron, folate, calcium and zinc. Another great nutrient that we have already covered in detail, omega-3, is found in salmon. Omega-3 will help develop both your baby's brain and eyes, and can easily be obtained through eating this yummy fish. While mercury may be a concern, salmon is listed as a low-mercury fish, meaning you can ingest up to 12 ounces of it a week without worrying about negative effects. Salmon can be prepared in many healthy ways, such as being grilled or broiled, and it can be easily added into pastas and salads.

Though you never want to eat them raw or undercooked, eggs are a great, easy source of amino acids. Amino acids will help a baby's growth alongside other nutrients found in an egg. Eggs contain more than a dozen vitamins and minerals. One of these is choline, which can help with early brain development. Berries are another good source of vitamins that can be put into many different dishes, but they have the added bonus of not having to be cooked. Just as with beans, the type of berry, be it blackberry, blueberry or raspberry, does not matter. All berries contain a certain amount of vitamin C, potassium as well as folate and fiber. They also go great with the final food on this list, low-fat yogurt. While you may not think it, yogurt has more calcium than milk, and is very high in protein. This, in combination with how easy it is to mix it with other healthy choices like fruit and cereal, make it one of the best inclusions into your new diet.

Now that we have covered some good foods to eat throughout your pregnancy, we will get into more specific detail about when is the best time to eat certain foods. For example, bananas, a great pregnancy food due to their vitamin C and potassium, are perfect for the early weeks of pregnancy due to their ability to offset nausea. Spinach, one of the classic greens, is also very good for the first trimester due to its folate content. Folate is very essential to the first weeks of pregnancy to prevent neural tube defects, which harm the developing brain and spinal cord. As the fetus grows, it can put pressure on your uterus which can cause constipation. The fiber content of beans fights this constipation, making them very useful in the first trimester as well. The last good food for the early weeks, red bell peppers, are strong as they have a much higher vitamin C content than other fruits and vegetables. Vitamin C is always good to have during pregnancy, but its ability to repair tissues makes it especially good for the beginning.

The second trimester is when the fetus really begins to develop. As such, this is where you want to focus your egg eating to make sure you intake a good amount of choline, which helps develop the brain. To do this, focus on the yolk more than the whites. If you do not eat eggs, soy is a good replacement, as are beef and milk. Avocados are also a great choice for the second trimester. They have many nutrients that help with brain and tissue growth, while also providing you with fiber, vitamin K, folate, vitamin C, potassium, B6 as well as mono-unsaturated fats. The calcium and protein in yogurt also make it a good snack during this time.

For the final trimester you want to make sure to put papaya, nuts and fatty fish into your diet. The benefits of fatty fish and omega-3's have already been explained, but papaya and nuts can be very important to this last stage. Papaya has a lot of nutrients (vitamin C, potassium, folate) that can help regulate heartburn, which is much more common during the third trimester. Just make sure the papaya you eat is always ripe. Nuts, on the other hand, are good due to their ability to be a healthy snack. As discomfort continues to grow into the third trimester, it is important to eat often. Nuts are great for this, as they also supply you with extra amounts of vitamins and nutrients you need to thrive.

25. Avoiding Anxiety-Triggering Situations

Though it may sound rather straightforward, the best way to diffuse distress during pregnancy is to avoid problems that cause distress. Distress, be it depression, stress or anxiety, happens naturally at all different times during the pregnancy process. This comes from many different sources in a lot of different ways. While you can do many things to prevent these things, nothing is more effective than trying as best you can to simply avoid distress-causing situations altogether.

The number one form of distress you want to avoid, as it can have negative ramifications on both your body and mind, are panic attacks. Despite all the prevention techniques, panic attacks are still seen to occur in 10 percent of women during their pregnancy period. The symptoms of these attacks are the same they would be in any other panic attack: shortness of breath, shaking, increased heartbeat, chest pain and dizziness. Naturally, these should be avoided as best they can, and nothing achieves this better thnn avoidance of stressful situations.

Now, while it is easy to say, this process is not always as easy as it sounds. Research shows that women who already have a history of panic attacks are more likely to experience them during pregnancy, and some people are more prone to these attacks if they occur in other members of their family. During pregnancy, the risk and regularity of these attacks is much higher than it normally would be no matter what your history with attacks. Both stress and anxiety, such as worrying about the pregnancy itself or the future of your baby, can trigger attacks, as can anything as simple as being overheated or uncomfortable. Even drinking coffee that is too hot can set off an attack. This simplicity shows how difficult these situations can be to avoid.

Though no one knows for sure, many speculate that panic attacks can also be triggered through hormonal levels, which are in constant fluctuation during pregnancy. However, more often than not they are brought on by thinking. Negative thoughts or worries about the future are very common triggers, as each can lead a pregnant women to start to freak out over her situation. These panic attacks are worrisome, as they can impact the fetus, causing a restriction of blood flow that has been linked to prematurity or low-birth weight. However, many of the relaxation techniques in this guide, in combination with many of the wellness techniques, can help battle this.

As stated, avoiding any situations that may bring on stress is the best way to avoid these panic attacks. If you start to feel uncomfortable or uneasy remove yourself from where you are and get to a more comfortable area. If the attacks are being triggered by something mental, such as thinking, you may want to seek outside help. Cognitive therapy is one such method that helps with this. Cognitive therapy is a great form of help that teaches you to take bad thoughts and replace them with much more positive thinking. This is commonly used in practice with behavioral therapy, which incorporates many of the mindfulness techniques seen in section one. These techniques help pregnant women better avoid stress by teaching them to focus on the now and forget about the future to come.

Each of the above methods give you much more control over your thoughts, which can help immensely in the reduction of stress. Reducing stress is the main way to stop yourself from having panic attacks, which makes these methods so essential. Deep breathing and other relaxation techniques can also be very helpful when trying to overcome your anxiety.

As always, you should also never rule out talking to your doctor if you suffer from continued attacks or your attempts to fix them are not working. Medication can be implemented as a way to help relieve stress associated with attacks, but you should always be careful when dealing with any type of medication during pregnancy. Discuss it with your doctor before deciding to use any form of medication, and always do your own research on what effects it could have on your body. Therapy mixed with relaxation techniques is often enough to stem the tide, but in the cases where this will not work, consulting a physician is a fine route.

26. Keep An Active Social Life

While pregnancy can be an exhilarating and exciting time for any woman, it can also be very isolating. Staying at home, keeping to yourself and excessive sleeping are all habits that you can develop during this time. None of these are healthy, and avoiding these tendencies is a good idea for any pregnant women. A social life is a good way to fight these habits. Maintaining a good social life is important throughout the time you are pregnant, and it has many benefits pertaining to the alleviation of distress.

Just know, exhaustion will come. It is an integral part of the pregnancy process, and is bound to happen to anyone going through such a taxing time. However, while sleep is beneficial (and necessary) you typically want to try to get out of the house when the opportunity arises. When looking to have an increase in your social life, there are two avenues you can take. One option is spending time and doing activities with your partner, which makes sense since they are around more than other people. Another good way to make sure you keep an active social life is through spending times with your friends. Such people not only are able to bring you out into the world and keep you from staying isolated, but they also serve as great support systems to have during difficult times.

Use these people to make sure you stay active. This can mean a variety of different things, and won't be the same for every woman. Just remember, while being social is very important, you don't need to do a lot to make sure you are being active. Wallowing or inactivity has negative ramifications to your mental health, and doing something as simple as going to eat or watching a movie can give you the proper stimulation you need to avoid falling into a bad place.

In conjunction with spending more time with your loved ones, bonding with your spouse is a very important part of this socialization process. Your partner is a very important part of your pregnancy. Besides sharing your child, they also share in the overall process as well. They are a wonderful support system, and they will help to make your time better. As such, you want to connect with them as much and as deeply as possible. This bonding with your partner can foster a deeper, healthier connection.

Bonding with your partner is the most important factor of creating a proper social life. Not only is your partner a great, essential piece to helping you through the pregnancy process, but a good connection will enable both of you to transition more smoothly into the post-pregnancy period. Pregnancy is not a process that you have to go alone. Always try to involve your partner into the process when you can, as it can help you in many ways. A shared project, such as the simple of act of going to the movies, is a great way to foster this connection. Vacations are another very strong way to help you both relax and stimulate a healthy environment for you and your partner. No matter the levels of exhaustion in your life, always try to spend as much time with them as you can.

A social life beyond your partner also has plenty of benefits, and is one of the more overlooked elements to a successful pregnancy. Nine months is a long time, there's no denying that, but the process can seem even longer when you are spending it alone. As with so many tips and tools in this guide, try to always be aware of the world around you. If you are sulking or find yourself being isolated from your friends and family, make a conscious effort to do things with them. Get out when you can, and try to avoid general inactivity. These little things will greatly help you in the long run, and give you the amounts of mental stability you need in addition to bettering your mood.

27. The Benefits of a Warm Bath

Another proper relaxation tool you can utilize as a form of self-therapy is taking a bath. Bathing is a very simple solution that can solve many problems. Not only that, but it is very easy to accomplish due to its ability to be so easily incorporated into your daily routines. Bathing is a great form of therapy for any pregnant women, and can be helpful during all times of the process. As with everything else, there are some things you should know about proper bathing techniques, and they will follow.

One benefit to taking a bath is that you can add your own ingredients and oils to the water. Similar to aromatherapy, these oils can have soothing or positive effects on both your body and the health of your growing baby. All of these oils have different effects, and will help you in different ways. If you are suffering from anxiety, for example, there are numerous bath oils can help reduce its effects. Lemon and lavender are two examples of such oils you can use, but there are a plethora of different kinds that can benefit you depending on the effects that you most need.

At some point, you may have heard mixed theories on whether or not you should bathe during pregnancy. This is understandable, as it was a topic of debate a few years ago. However, at this point in time, it is generally accepted that baths are beneficial to pregnant women. Still, there is a right and wrong way to go about bathing. Doing it the right way can lead to a much healthier pregnancy, while the wrong way has been shown to put extra stress on the mother as well as the newborn.

Bathing is a great relaxant, and can be very important in fostering your baby's early development. However, there are numerous factors you should be aware of when trying to take a bath. If these rules are followed, and the entire process goes according to plan, then these baths can be a very good way to work a natural anxiety reducer into your lifestyle.

The most important rule to follow when deciding to take a bath is to never allow the water to get hotter than 98 degrees Fahrenheit. While hot water can be very soothing on muscles and cramps, especially the ones that occur during this time, having water that is either too hot or overheated can be very bad for the fetus, as water that is too hot can restrict blood flow to your growing baby. This reduction of blood then puts the baby under a large amount of stress, which can have many negative effects such as causing problems with development. Anything over the 98 degree threshold is considered harmful, while anything under it should be fine (though you might want to go a few degrees lower). The best way to keep control of this, especially if you are someone who loves to take baths, is to purchase a bath thermometer.

During your bath there are a couple of other factors that you want to be aware of. One of these concerns is the added risk of infection. Infection is something that should always be actively avoided during the months of pregnancy, and that risk has the ability to increase when you bathe. These typically apply to vaginal infections, which have the ability to occur when you are in water for long periods of time. However, such infections are easily preventable. If you want to take a quick dip into a warm tub, just make sure it doesn't last too long. Thirty minutes in the water is a good time frame to follow, but sitting in the tub for hours is not recommended, as this allows a prime environment for the infection to occur.

Despite some of the risks, bathing can be very good for a pregnant mother. Soaking in warm water has the ability to reduce the swelling of both arms and legs, which then reduces muscle pain. Amniotic fluids can also increase as the result of taking a bath. Bathing is good at preventing premature contractions which are known to be very painful. Bathing also aids relaxation, and will put your mind at ease, which reduces anxiety. So, if you do enjoy baths, or if you find that they help with some of your symptoms, then keep on bathing. Just make sure to be responsible when you do, and add some oils while you're at it.

28. Vacation Days

This next section will deal with work. Or, more accurately, ways to avoid it. We have, in numerous sections, gone over the potential setbacks of extra stress, which includes anxiety and panic attacks. If this stress builds, it can even spread to cause complications with your baby. As such, it is a good idea to keep as calm as possible during your nine months. Resisting distress is very important to this, and work can bring on some unwanted stress. As such, you should try to use vacation days during your pregnancy as a way to alleviate some of the stress that comes from work.

Managing your vacation days happens in two different sections. The first of these is to properly plan before your pregnancy begins, while the second is how to effectively use vacation days as a form of relaxation once your pregnancy happens. It does not matter what your job is, work can always add some extra pressure during your pregnancy. If you need to work throughout the nine months, just be aware of how much you are working, and the type of stress it is putting on your life. No matter how you work, chances are you are going to need to take some time off at one point or another. How much time you take off depends on how exactly your job is effecting you, but always take work off when you need it.

Vacation days can be really central to properly help you prepare for the coming pregnancy. If you do plan on becoming pregnant, try to save or accumulate the most amount of vacation days that you can in preparation for the event. Extra days can wait, as can vacations. Your vacation days are very important to maintaining health during pregnancy, and they can help both your mentality as well as your physicality. They become even more important as you move towards the later trimesters, where your body will be in its biggest stages of fluctuation. The more days you can afford to use for rest, the easier it will be to keep up with your pregnancy.

During the actual pregnancy is the time when you want to start using those sick days that you have accumulated. Listen to your body, and make sure to quit if you are working too hard or feel yourself becoming sick or agitated. Stress should be avoided at all costs. You don't necessarily have to take weeks off at a time, but you want to sprinkle your vacation days throughout all nine months according to when you need them. Using a vacation day during the middle or end of the week can really help you during a tough time, and push you to the weekend. Even just taking an afternoon off, especially if you had a particularly hard morning, can be very good to keep your mental health in place. Being tired is something that happens more and more often as you move through your pregnancy, and you want to offset this as much as possible. A day off can help just as much toward your health as getting the right amount of sleep.

A big part of pregnancy is learning to be able to take other people's help. There is nothing wrong seeking other people's council, and you should use your support systems as much as possible. Learning to slow down and rest is something that you are going to have to do, especially as you move into the second or third trimester. During this time, don't forget to use yourself as a support system as well. Using sick days just to take some time for yourself can be very beneficial to relaxing your mind. Never think or expect to do it all on your own. Yes, things can happen, and yes work can be very important, but if you need to go home and rest, or if you just need some time to yourself, don't be afraid to take these vacation days. They exist for a reason, and you should use them accordingly.

29. Avoiding Negative Thoughts

One of the last points we will cover in this guide is a topic that has been touched upon, but never completely examined, through many of the previous sections: mindset. Mental health is extremely key in pregnancy, and becomes even more so after your child is born. One rule that you should live by during and beyond the nine months is, stay positive. Positivity can go an extremely long way, and can make it so you stay both happy and healthy. Your health directly affects your newborn as it grows, and the results of staying positive, or rather the detriments that come from being negative, can impact their health in a very large way.

The first, and most important, part of staying positive is to understand that it starts with yourself. Just as with the wellness practices outlined in section two, you need have a high level of self-awareness, which will keep you in the best mindset possible. All fear, negativity, anxiety and stress stems from somewhere. You can overcome all of those problems by being aware of where exactly they are coming from.

Negative feelings are usually sparked by the "scary story", which refers to a pregnancy complication that has been either told to you or that you have told yourself. "Scary story" can also pertain to negative thoughts or a negative incident that you tell yourself of during pregnancy, such as that you will be a terrible mother. The best way to confront such thoughts is to meet them head on. Know these scenarios, no matter how frightening, aren't going to happen. Rationalizing such thoughts will help you understand how irrational these fears are. Even if these scary stories do happen, know you are strong enough to battle them. If such problems ever arise, the best way to battle them is through positive thoughts and calm thinking. Panicking is never an appropriate response to any complication.

Another good tip for maintaining strong mental health is, stay in the present. Every scary story or fear you build or think about will happen in the future tense. This is because none of these scenarios have happened, and are unlikely to come true. The more you think about these stories, the more daunting they can become. The stress that comes from such thinking is very unhealthy for both you and your baby. To avoid this, try and focus your mind on other, more positive aspects about your life. Things can always go wrong, but if you live in the present, and know that currently everything is fine, you will do a great job of restricting stress that comes from this type of thinking.

Earlier we discussed that you should never forget to use yourself as a support system. This is very important to living a healthy life, and can be utilized here as a form of positive self-talk. People who often suffer from depression or anxiety have very negative self-talk. That is, they focus on negative parts of life rather than the more positive. Examples of this negative self-talk are, "I can't do this", "I can't handle this", "What if I fail?", "What if something terrible happens?" or "what if it doesn't work?". Try to avoid this type of thinking when you can, and stick to positive thinking with phrases such as "I can do this" and "I can handle whatever comes my way". The first batch of sentences fuel bad feelings, while the second are much more empowering and beneficial to a positive attitude.

Positive thoughts can instill a lot of confidence in yourself regarding pregnancy, and keep you away from dark or harmful places. Remember, negative thinking leads to many complications that can be harmful to your growing baby. Most negativity that occurs during pregnancy is based off of worrying about things that haven't happened, and most likely won't. As long as you understand and face your fears head on, you will be able to rise above these dark thoughts.

Don't waste your time on what if's. Yes, there are a thousand scary scenarios and complications that could happen during your pregnancy, but they rarely ever happen. Thinking or focusing on such things serves no purpose but to further any anxiety or fear you might be feeling. Remember, just as bad things can happen, they can just as easily not happen. Self-awareness is a good method to implement during these times in order to foster the proper mindset. Notice why you are spending so much time on what if's, and then use that thinking to understand how they are harmful to your mood. Realization is very important to keeping a positive attitude, and this, mixed with the good thoughts that sit at the center of positive self-talk, are what create a solid, healthy mindset.

30. Cut Back on Your Workload

Pregnancy is a time in your life where you have to be honest with yourself. This involves understanding both your capabilities and your limitations. However, the most important part of that understanding is being aware that you can't do it all on your own. Just as work can add to your levels of stress and anxiety, doing other common tasks can increase that as well. It is common to experience frustration at not being able to operate as you once did. However, reducing your workload, both at home and work, is one of the best ways to try and keep your stress levels low.

Reducing the amount of work you do can happen in various ways. The first of these is at your job. When trying to work during your pregnancy, be aware of the extra stress that it can cause. Never push yourself too far, and try to work a schedule that bests suits you. If you can manage, it is often good to only work part-time during your pregnancy, especially as you move into the later trimesters. In conjunction with this idea, if you get asked to work overtime or extra hours, you should often politely decline. This time in your life is for focusing on your baby, and work should come second to that.

A lighter workload can also help you reduce stress. Stress, as you now know, is at the center of many problems that pregnancy brings. As such, you want to always find ways to alleviate stress. Cutting back on your overall workload, both at your job and in general life, is a great way to achieve this. This time in your life should be focused on yourself and giving your baby the best start possible. If you need to take breaks, do it when you can. Any type of reduction to your normal work can go a long way. Even something as simple as basic chores or your normal household tasks. Clean spaces are conducive to a healthy mind, but if your home is cluttered, ask your partner to perform these tasks; especially if you are feeling tired or not up to the task.

You never want to push yourself too far in any part of your pregnancy, and work is at the forefront of this mindset. Many women who experience pregnancy have difficulties breaking from their set habits. Just know if you feel in a similar way that it is perfectly natural to let some things go. Another way to fight stress-building habits is to choose which battles (fighting with you partner, boss, kids etc.) you want to fight. Being angry or in a spat also increases stress and uses energy, which should be saved as much as possible.

Another method that can be helpful when you are trying to avoid stress is to stay away from any "information overload". That is to say, don't try and take in all of your pregnancy information at one time. Just as with this guide, pregnancy is a learning process. Taking it slow will help you tackle your problems one at a time, which makes them easier to deal with. By doing this, you can compartmentalize the entire process of pregnancy, which makes it easier to deal with as a whole.

Working too much, or trying to work too much, can be detrimental to a successful pregnancy. Typically, it is best, even if you are not used to it, to try to do as little as possible. Your number one priority is your baby, and the fetus will benefit from you getting as much rest as possible. Extra rest will also help you go about your daily life. Being restricted may be irritating at first, but understand that a more relaxing lifestyle is essential to having the most successful pregnancy possible.

31. Go to the Spa

The last section in this guide will cover one final way you can make your pregnancy process easier, and that is going to the spa. As the above section discussed, pregnancy should primarily seen as a time of relaxation where you can focus on your own needs. Getting some time at the spa can be perfect for this, and many of them have special arrangements set up for women who are undergoing pregnancy.

The best time to go to a spa during pregnancy is usually during the second trimester. This is crucial period because it both is beyond morning sickness, and serves as a point in the pregnancy where you should be experiencing a bit more energy. In terms of your body, it also is the safest time to take full advantage of the number of different ways a spa can help you relax. Certain spas even suggest that pregnant women shouldn't undergo treatments until they are between 12 and 32 week into their pregnancy.

Spas are beneficial for two key reasons. On one hand, they can help you with any ailments you might be feeling. On the other, they also allow you some much needed time to yourself. Typically, it is best for you to find a spa that specializes in treating pregnant women. When you make an appointment, let them know you are pregnant, as that will give them time to make the proper accommodations.

When seeking ways to reduce physical stress, explore the many great treatments spas offer for your body. Massages can work wonders for your back and joints, while also giving aid to your hips and legs. If you use a spa that has treatments for pregnant women, they may have certain gear or equipment that can make your trip even easier. Also, if you find that you are particularly susceptible to smells, be sure to tell them to use unscented oils.

When at the spa, you may also want to indulge in a facial. Facials are a great form of relaxation, but your skin is generally more sensitive during this time. As such, any facial ingredients you used before may not be good for you now. The most common ingredient you want to avoid is retinoid; a type of vitamin A that can speed up cell division. In small doses it isn't particularly worrisome, but when used a lot it can harm your baby. Nail polish, used in both manicures and pedicures, similarly should only be used in small doses. Using these products in larger doses can be harmful, as they contain the chemicals formaldehyde and toluene. These can cause irritation to your throat, lungs and eyes. Toluene, when used in large amounts, can also cause problems with your baby. To mitigate the amount of risk, try and avoid the nail bar during the first trimester.

The above treatments are some of the great ways spas help foster relaxation. However, there are also parts of the spa that you should try to avoid. Overheating, for instance, is not good for your baby. This means you want to typically avoid heat treatments, which includes saunas, hot tubs, baths, hot springs, tanning beds and stream rooms. Warm water should also be avoided but, just as with bathing at home, a quick dip isn't going to cause much harm. Those are the ways a spa can help you, and many different ways to cope with the pregnancy process. Use the methods laid out in this guide to the best of your ability, experiment with them based on any problems you might be having, and find which ones work best for you.

Printed in Great Britain
by Amazon.co.uk, Ltd.,
Marston Gate.